W9-CSU-732

PRO TACTICS™

FISHING BASS
TOURNAMENTS

PRO TACTICS™ SERIES

PRO TACTICS™

FISHING BASS TOURNAMENTS

*Use the Secrets of the Pros to
Compete Successfully*

David E. Dirks

THE LYONS PRESS
Guilford, Connecticut
An imprint of The Globe Pequot Press

To buy books in quantity for corporate use
or incentives, call **(800) 962–0973**
or e-mail **premiums@GlobePequot.com**.

Copyright © 2009 Morris Book Publishing, LLC

ALL RIGHTS RESERVED. No part of this book may be reproduced or transmitted in any form by any means, electronic or mechanical, including photocopying and recording, or by any information storage and retrieval system, except as may be expressly permitted in writing from the publisher. Requests for permission should be addressed to The Globe Pequot Press, Attn: Rights and Permissions Department, P.O. Box 480, Guilford, CT 06437.

The Lyons Press is an imprint of The Globe Pequot Press.
Pro Tactics is a trademark of Morris Book Publishing, LLC.

Text design by Peter Holm (Sterling Hill Productions) and Libby Kingsbury

Library of Congress Cataloging-in-Publication Data

Dirks, David E.
  Fishing bass tournaments : use the secrets of the pros to compete
successfully / David E. Dirks.
      p. cm.
  At head of title: Pro Tactics
  ISBN 978-1-59921-423-8
  1. Bass fishing. 2. Tournament fishing. I. Title. II. Title: Pro
Tactics.
  SH681.D57 2009
  799.17'73—dc22
                                        2008028259
Printed in China

10 9 8 7 6 5 4 3 2 1

The author and The Globe Pequot Press assume no liability for accidents happening to, or injuries sustained by, readers who engage in the activities described in this book.

This book is dedicated to my loving and patient family as well as the thousands of competitive anglers who enjoy bass fishing to such an extent that they dedicate a good portion of their lives to increasing their knowledge and then sharing it with others.

It is also dedicated to the six professional bass anglers and especially their families, who do without them for most of the year: Paul Elias, Randy Howell, Jimmy Mason, Frank Scalish, Terry Scroggins, and Sam Swett.

■ Terry Scroggins uses a release tool to safely unhook a fish.
LURENET.COM

CONTENTS

ACKNOWLEDGMENTS

This book wouldn't have been possible had it not been for the help I received from my good friend Ken Schultz. One of America's most prolific fishing writers, it was Ken who took the time to send me the info on this book project. He also provided invaluable contacts and advice that enabled me to put this book together. I am deeply indebted to Ken.

There are six anglers who contributed an average of five hours on the telephone or in person for in-depth interviews, and this book is based entirely on their personal and professional experiences on the bass tournament trail. Terry Scroggins, Frank Scalish, Jimmy Mason, Paul Elias, Sam Swett, and Randy Howell are among the best of the best. They held nothing back and freely shared their strategies and tactics with me.

Jeff Samsel from PRADCO enabled me to meet many of the pros in person for interviews, research, and anything else I needed. He gave generously and with heart.

Special thanks to Kelly Barefoot of Custom Lures Unlimited for sharing his expansive knowledge of bass lure design and providing custom lures used for photography for this book.

TJ Stallings from TTI Companies and Dave Washburn from the FLW Tour provided access to additional pro anglers and much in the way of resources for this book. Thanks also to Tommy Akin of Akin Promotions for sharing his public relations expertise with me and Scott Rauber for sharing his expertise on marketing to tour sponsors.

Last but certainly not least, a big thank-you to my editor, Bill Schneider. Through his advice and guidance, I've learned much more about the art, the craft, and the business of writing.

Winning Bass Tournaments

This book doesn't teach Bass Fishing 101. It's more like Winning Bass Tournaments 101, and it's based on the well-honed experiences of real bass professionals. These are folks whose livelihoods rely on how well they do or do not do in any particular tournament. Winning bass tournaments at the BASS or FLW level is business. With millions in prize money awarded to thousands of anglers each year, this is a big-business operation. Tournament bass fishing is at the epicenter of the growing popularity of bass fishing around the country.

No doubt, freshwater fishing is a major industry. According to the National Sportfishing Association, freshwater fishing generates more than $114 billion annually in total economic output—that translates to slightly over one million jobs. It's estimated that nearly 30 percent of that annual economic output, or about $34.2 billion, comes from bass fishing alone.

Found in more waters and in more geographies than any other freshwater fish, bass—which includes largemouth, smallmouth, and spotted—are the kings of freshwater sport fish. In a June 2007 survey of 1,138 freshwater anglers by Southwick Associates, Inc., nearly 92 percent reported targeting largemouth, smallmouth, or spotted bass. Of those, 79 percent were fishing with artificial baits. Truly, bass fishing in America is an immense segment of the fishing business and is almost an industry in and of itself.

The competitive bass-fishing segment has developed momentum of its own. The 2008 BASS Elite Series is offering more than $7.5 million in cash prizes spread out among eleven events. In each of these eleven events, the first-place pro angler takes a check of $100,000. The lowest payout, for the fiftieth-place pro angler finish, is $10,000. The Bassmaster Angler of the Year pays $250,000 alone, with the second-place finisher taking home a mere $100,000. And if you're good enough to make the most competitive of all tournaments, the Bassmaster Classic, and you have a first-place win, you can take a check for $500,000 (based on 2008 payouts).

Not to be left out, weekend bass warriors can fish the Bassmaster Weekend series, with events held all across the country each year. The payouts for weekend

■ **Working with the press is a requirement, not an option, when you're a touring pro. Pro Tim Horton works with a photographer during a photo shoot.** DAVID DIRKS

tournaments are considerably less than the professional series, from a top payout of $13,000 (first place) all the way down to $200 (fortieth place). Of course, that doesn't include bonus money and prizes that can bring in up to $10,000 in additional winnings.

The FLW Tour represents even more money for competitive bass-angling professionals. In 2007 Scott Suggs was the first professional bass angler ever to win $1 million during the FLW Forrest Wood Cup competition. The total prize money distributed during this one FLW tournament was $2 million. It's definitely big-time bass fishing.

Each year thousands of bass clubs in almost every state host competitions on their local and statewide bass waters. These tournaments are usually based on winning points and, in many cases, prize money. Mostly one-day tournaments, the first prize can range from $100 up to $700 or $800. It's not big money, but the competition is just as intense as at the pro tournaments.

So what does all this tell us? It means there is no end to the number of tournament

■ Pro Randy Howell understands what it feels like under the hot lights of tournament drama. Before the lights go on, he spends hours preparing for a moment like this. DAVID DIRKS

opportunities available for the amateur, semiprofessional, and professional bass angler. And with the encouragement of junior bass clubs and tournaments, a new generation of bass anglers is on the rise.

As with any large participation-oriented sport, bass fishing has no lack of books, magazines, television programs, instructional DVDs, and podcasts dedicated to educating bass anglers of all levels. Typing "bass fishing" in the search box of a leading online bookseller reveals 3,859 results for bass books. On top of this you can add in hundreds of instructional videos, 445,000

search results for bass-fishing blogs, 95,800 results for podcasts, and millions of Web pages full of everything related to bass fishing.

So how do you win bass tournaments consistently? If Kevin VanDam says that he used lure X to win, the next-day sales of lure X will surely shoot up. That's great for the tackle industry but not enough to help you win more tournaments. If buying the "winning" bait was all it took to win or at least place high enough to get a check, then everyone would catch fish. It just isn't so.

■ **Terry Scroggins (right) shares a lighter moment with fellow pro angler Tim Horton during tournament practice.** DAVID DIRKS

Some folks would say that winning or losing in tournament fishing is luck. I don't believe this is true. Someone once told me that luck is the point where preparation meets opportunity. When they intersect, a tournament win cannot be far off.

Every angler in the Bassmaster or FLW professional tours excels at bass fishing. You don't get to turn pro unless you have proven yourself at some level against a field of excellent anglers. There are no "average" anglers in that professional competitive field, and it's been said that every angler in it has the same chance to win as everyone else.

There is more to tournament fishing than most people hear or see, and most of it is not at all as glamorous as what you see during the final weigh-in of a Bassmaster or FLW tournament. What you see on television is the end result of a professional who spends countless hours engaged in research, preparation, practice,

strategy and tactics, and, most important, decision-making.

To find out what it takes to be a successful bass tournament angler at any level, I talked with six bass professionals. In hours of interviews, we discussed what no camera shows and most books never discuss at any great length. We delved into the work behind the scenes that is required to prepare for and win tournaments. And yes, each pro shared his best tournament presentations and the baits he uses, and this information is also included in these pages. No bass book would be complete without that.

This book isn't built on what *I* think it takes to successfully prepare for and fish a bass tournament, nor is it your typical bass book. It's built on the words of pros like Terry Scroggins, Randy Howell, Frank Scalish, Paul Elias, Jimmy Mason, and Sam Swett—all of whom have earned the right to be called "bass professionals."

CHAPTER ONE

Pretournament Research

Professional bass anglers on just about every tour, be it BASS or FLW, invest some time before each tournament researching the water they will be fishing. Unless you've been on the tour for twenty-five years and have fished a lake fifty-six times in every season under every condition possible, pretournament research is a big key to winning, or at least cashing a check. Well before the tackle is organized, baits are checked, boats are readied, and the trucks are loaded, top

▮ Jimmy Mason does the unglamorous but important work of checking and organizing baits before a tournament. DAVID DIRKS

■ Make sure you have all the gear you want to bring with you before you leave for a tournament. DAVID DIRKS

bass professionals are doing their homework. It's not glamorous, but it's part of the business.

The investment of time into pretournament research has many benefits. Key among them:

- It gives you a chance to become familiar with a body of water well before you arrive, which saves you time and money. Knowing what gear to bring and what kinds of conditions you'll find in that season improves your ability to keep yourself organized.
- You'll discover what you didn't know about the water. The more you peel that lake or river back, the more you realize you need to know about it.
- Researching a body of water and answering critical questions about its character will open up more questions. By asking more questions, you'll gain a perspective about the water and how you can prepare and fish it successfully.
- Research helps you eliminate unproductive water. Some tournaments are held on gigantic bodies of water. There isn't enough time to check the entire lake, so research can help you eliminate unproductive areas sooner. This leaves you with a better setup for your practice time.
- Pretournament research will put you competitively ahead of anglers who didn't bother to spend the time. You'll

already have a huge advantage over those who think their skills and experience will be enough to lead them to victory.

SOME KEY QUESTIONS TO ASK ABOUT A BODY OF WATER AS YOU CONDUCT YOUR RESEARCH

- What parts of the lake seem to be producing in recent tournaments?
- What kinds of vegetation are available and where are they located?
- At what depths are the fish suspended?
- What are the water temperatures of the lake in the season?
- What is the water clarity?
- What is the water level of the lake?
- What kinds of lure trends have won the tournament? What was the bait that won the tournament?
- What has been the weather pattern in the area very recently?
- What is the weather forecast for the next several weeks?
- What weight of fish has it taken to win a tournament recently?
- What have been the average daily weights of fish on this lake?

Researching Maps

No self-respecting, successful tournament angler goes to a competitive event without reviewing either an electronic or paper map of the lake or river. Most tournament victories are built on the foundation of a well-worn, marked-up map. It's a tool that can help you figure out where you don't want to fish during practice, and a well-annotated map can help you find potential spots for bass when your practice has not gone well. If you capture enough information with it, it becomes the living history of a body of water. Seasonal influences,

special situations, drawings of structure not printed on the map, and other nuances of the water and the fish can be noted for current and future tournaments.

Frank Scalish: "My favorite thing is a map. A good map will tell you a lot. Today, with [electronics], you have tools that weren't even dreamed of when I first started fishing. I'm a structure fisherman by love and addiction, and if I found rock piles, I used to remember them by cross-triangulation. I had notebooks and notebooks of information on lakes. Maps are important but not always accurate. They

■ The lake maps available today are full of detailed information about the water. Adding your own notes provides a rich database of tournament information.
DAVID DIRKS

can give you a basic idea of where to look.

"I'll have five or six maps for each lake. I was fishing Lake Hartwell years ago and had never fished it before. It was a Jerry Rind tournament. I'd catch a few fish and then not catch anything for a while. This repeated itself all during the day. Armed with my map and GPS, I discovered that every time I was catching a fish, the pattern was inside channel bends and riprap. The next day I went from catching fish every now and then to catching them all day long. It was an incredible pattern."

Jimmy Mason: "The first thing I do at the beginning of the [tournament] year is order all the maps for each lake. I like to order different maps for the same lake because there are times when you'll see something on one map that will not be on the others, so it's good to see a variety of maps.

"If I'm fishing a TVA [Tennessee Valley Authority] or Army Corps of Engineers lake, I'll order a set of the government maps. They are some of the most detailed.

The TVA maps are some of the best for those TVA lakes. I'll usually end up with two or three maps per lake.

"Using maps allows me to get the big picture of how far everything is apart on the lake. If you're looking at, say, secondary points on a creek, you can look around and get a bigger view of other creeks that might have similar points."

Terry Scroggins: For Scroggins, there's a world of difference between the pretournament research he did when he started competitive bass fishing and now: "Once you go to all these reservoirs, lakes, and rivers four or five times each, you start to learn them."

While he had used hard-copy maps and other such tools in the early part of his career, he now relies on his Navionics package for the lake research he does before and during a tournament. "I use Lowrance electronics and the Navionics chips. With their mapping ability, it's like a 'live' map of the water. I really, really rely on that more than anything. . . . Once I

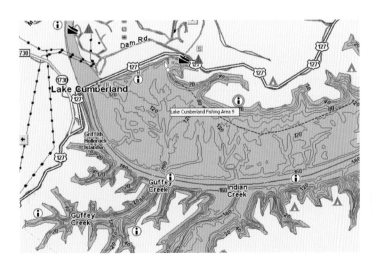

■ **Electronic lake maps have extraordinary detail, and almost every pro uses them today.**
DAVID DIRKS

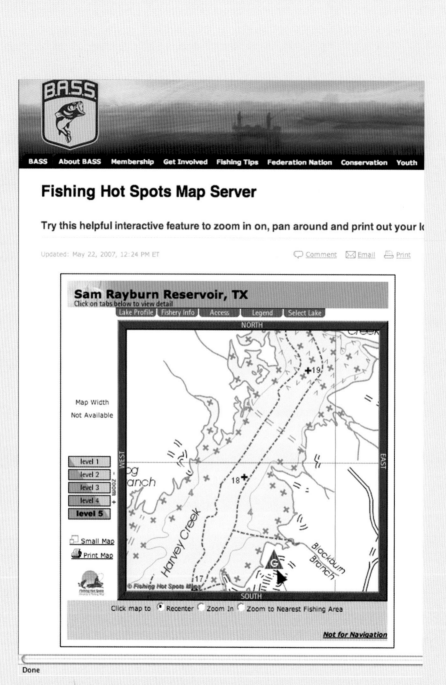

■ **Example of a free Internet map.** DAVID DIRKS

leave home [for a tournament], I use my Navionics chip because it's so detailed. I know it sounds really simple, but it's showing you everything you need to know as you're driving across the lake."

Scroggins views the technology and mapping as only a way to get started and not enough to win a tournament. Given that most everyone on the tournament trail has access to electronic mapping software these days, it takes more than good mapping skills to win.

Internet Research

The World Wide Web has brought an explosion of information on bass, recreational bass fishing, and competitive bass fishing. While there are literally thousands of books available on bass fishing and many fine bass magazines, the Internet has created a deep well of information and data from a vast number of recreational anglers, tournament anglers, and a multitude of bass-related companies. A search on the Web for "tournament bass fishing" brings up 381,000 results, and "bass fishing" alone results in a whopping 6,550,000 results. Enter "Terry Scroggins" and you get 86,500 results. Want more information on Lake Amistad? That will net you about 48,700 results. You get the picture.

Will you sort through 6,550,000 results, or even 48,700? Of course you aren't. If your search results are in the millions, your search is too broad. Here are

some ways to sharpen your search and narrow it down to the most useful results:

- Use more than one word. One-word queries are just too broad for an Internet search.
- Drop common words like "the" and "it." Stick to your search target.
- If you're searching a specific phrase, put it in quotes. Typing "Terry Scroggins" inside quotation marks yields 6,010 results instead of 48,700.
- Use all lowercase letters to save time. There is no need to capitalize.

Scalish: Like many top pros, Scalish uses the Internet for pretournament research and recommends looking for recent local tournaments held on the lake you are going to fish. "I try to look for tournaments that have at least twenty-five to thirty boats because those are generally local tournaments. And then I look for tournaments with two hundred boats or more."

Scalish is looking for the "spread of weight" in those tournaments. "The most important thing to ask yourself is, what kinds of weights is this lake producing? Am I going to be OK catching 2-pounders, or do I need to catch 4-pounders? Is 10 pounds of weight per day good on this lake, or do I need 15? If you know the lake is capable of producing 11 pounds per day and you're catching 16 pounds during practice, you know you're going to be sitting in the top ten when it's all said and done."

■ **Sam Swett combines both paper maps and Google Earth mapping to find potential hot spots during his research.** SAM SWETT

While preparing for an upcoming tournament on Falcon Lake in Texas, Scalish found a previous tournament that was held about the same time as the one he was preparing for. "I found that they had 280 boats in this tournament, so I looked at how far down the list 20 pounds of weight went and found out that seventy-fifth place was 20.9 pounds and seventy-sixth place was 19.12 pounds. That tells me that 20 pounds a day is not going to give me a $10,000 check. By looking at that information, if I want to be in the top ten, I'm going to need 30

pounds of fish per day. I'll need 23 pounds per day just to make money. The winner of the previous tournament on Falcon Lake had nearly 50 pounds of fish per day! This is a spring tournament, so the weights were appropriate for that time of year."

Sam Swett: Swett uses Google Earth satellite imagery to show him a lot more of the lake than a paper map. With his paper map open in front of the computer screen, Swett will compare areas of the lake to what the satellite image shows. He may be able to see such areas as flooded trees or

▮ **Frank Scalish sets the hook on another quality fish during practice time.**
LURENET.COM

stumps and draw those onto his map. "I'm also looking at the lake levels. Is the lake flooded? How high is it flooded? I try to study the shoreline. Does it have timber that is flooded? Can I get my boat into the flooded farm pond near the lake? I'll put a question mark on the map if I'm not sure of the lake terrain and should verify it during practice. If for some reason I don't get the chance to pre-fish the lake, this process saves a lot of time."

If there is a lack of recent reports on a specific lake, Swett will look for Internet-

based reports on similar lakes nearby. It can give him hints as to what the bass are doing from a regional perspective.

Randy Howell: "Sometimes using the Internet, I can call someone with a fishing report whose name I've gotten off of a Web site and shoot the bull about what the lake looks like, what the water level is, and what typical patterns will be used during the season. I'll get most of the information that I want myself that way." He acknowledges that you still need to find your own fish and places to fish for them. "Finding

■ **Being able to fish in all kinds of cover and under all weather conditions is key to tournament success.** DAVID DIRKS

your own fish and using your own [fishing] strengths and ability will always pay more dividends than just getting a marked map from somebody and trying to fish somebody else's holes. It's knowing how to use information that you get that is the key more than anything else."

Howell also pays close attention to previous catch weights in recent tournaments. "That gives us an accurate read on what kinds of weights you'll need to catch to be competitive. With a thirty-day off-limits, where we can't talk to anybody

anyway, I'm relying on what I read on the Internet for tournament results."

In addition, Howell will try to find out where the predominant release area is on the lake or river. "Those areas are heavily stocked, weekend after weekend. That bass release area especially comes into play when you know there's been, say, a thousand bass let go in the past six weeks. Whether they stay in the boat ramp area or not, they're going to move around but not go more than 5 miles [from the release area]. To effectively fish those release areas, be sure to fish the boat ramp areas, the rip-rap leading up to the release areas, and the docks near the release area."

Seasonal Patterns and Weather

Bass are creatures of seasons. Their seasonal habits are well-known and have been documented in detail in countless bass books and magazines. Each season has its own special behavioral impact on bass. Springtime and early summer bring them up shallow to spawn, and fall and winter conspire to bring them back into the deep. While bass might be creatures of seasonal influence, that doesn't guarantee you anything. Seasonal patterns only give you a good starting point for building your fishing practice plan.

The greatest variable of all in tournament bass fishing is the weather, and it is also the variable that is well outside the control of any angler. It's entirely unpredictable at times, and the only sure thing is what the weather was yesterday. However, paying close attention to weather patterns within each season will help you become more effective at solving fishing problems and making good decisions.

Scalish: "The key is understanding seasonal patterns. You have to know what season it is in the place you're going to fish. Spring in Florida is winter in the Northeast. With an understanding of what seasonal pattern the lake you're going to fish is in and a map, you can eliminate three-quarters of the water available to fish [during a tournament]. The bass have to be in certain places dictated by the season. If you know it's spring, you know the fish are going to be near or at spawn. Looking at your map and studying the lake contour lines, you need to find the biggest flats on the lake. You'll need to concentrate on areas where the depth is 0 to 5 feet or 0 to 10 feet."

Scalish looks at the last three weeks of weather leading into the tournament. "I just want to see what the trends are. As for weather during a tournament, it's going to be what it's going to be. I don't worry too much about weather during a tournament."

Weather patterns in one area of the country versus another can sometimes have a different effect on the bass, Scalish notes. "In Florida, when a cold front hits, it's the worst thing that could ever happen to you. The bite in Florida goes to nothing in cold-front situations, but it's only in Florida that this seems to hold true. Where I live [near the Great Lakes], cold fronts don't mess the fish up. We have so many cold fronts that if the fish stopped eating every time one came in, they'd starve to death."

Mason: "One thing I do to learn the specific traits of a particular body of water is to review every *Bass Times* and *Bassmaster* magazine I have that relates to that specific water. I also have a good database of information on my computer for different bodies of water."

On his computer Mason has the results of every BASS tournament ever held, so he'll carefully check the results of those tournaments against the specific lake and season he's preparing for. He'll also check out what each of the top five anglers from the seasonal tournament specifically did to win, then analyze that information to see if any areas of the lake were mentioned often and what patterns were mostly used to win the top five. "I'm not looking for specific spots. Some lakes have different sections that are historically better than others. If you see many mentions of a particular arm of the lake over and over again, there must be a reason for that. Certain areas of a lake will turn on at different times than other areas, so you want to take that into consideration when you're considering places to start during practice."

During the prespawn in midspring, Mason looks outside spawning areas where the fish will be staging. "The fish will gang up as they prepare to move up to spawn. You're going to start your search in that mid-depth range of the lake. For example, in a clear-water lake, you should start fishing deeper than a stained-water lake.

"Bass are very basic—they live to spawn, eat, and survive. During the spring, they spawn. You can tailor your fishing around the stages of spawning: prespawn, spawn, and postspawn. In the fall, bass start feeding very heavily, following the shad back into the creeks, as they get stocked up for the winter. It's a very repeatable cycle that fish go through. You want to match the stage of the fish's life cycle they're in when you arrive at the lake [or river]."

Swett: On Oklahoma's Grand Lake, Swett's research on both the seasonal patterns and the weather patterns played into his success: "The week we arrived there, the temperature was 32 degrees. The next morning it was in the single digits, and it never got above 25 degrees for the rest of the week. Everybody was deepwater fishing, fishing a winter pattern. But the week before this tournament, it was in the 70-degree range. It was a very freak cold front that came through. The tournament was won on a buzzbait by Jim Morton, but I did very well on a spinnerbait. The reason why I threw a spinnerbait was because even though the surface water temperature was plummeting fast, the colder water was only a few inches deep. It's what I call an 'artificial surface temperature.' By studying the weather patterns and knowing what the average weather cycle was prior to the tournament, I knew that the water didn't have enough time to really turn over and get into a winter pattern.

Swett is always looking for common denominators. "Sometimes it's a lure. Other times it might be a location or a certain depth. You are trying to find a pattern, not necessarily specific spots. A lot of guys have the same information that you do. By digesting a lot of information and pulling out two or three common denominators, hopefully you can identify the right bait or the right section of the lake.

Local Anglers as a Resource: Buyer Beware!

It's logical to assume that anglers who live near and regularly fish tournament waters would be a great source of information for the competitive angler. Anglers who are fishing unfamiliar waters might be tempted to soak up as much local knowledge as they can get, but, like many things in life, too much of a "good thing" can kill you. Experienced bass anglers learn over time to pick and choose their sources of information carefully. They also know how to sift through the chaff to find those kernels of information that will help them round out their research on a body of water.

Scalish: "You can get very bad 'good' information from local anglers. Most local anglers are talking about [fishing] patterns that they experienced one or two times in their lifetime. They are usually not talking about patterns in the now. This is true unless it's a tournament that's taking place while you're there. Local anglers who live near a lake have a tendency to fish memories. They are sometimes unable to put together why they caught fish in a particular spot. Pattern fishing puts fish in your boat, and patterns will change and the fish will move on.

"If I tell you where to find fish and you don't catch them there, you'll have no idea how to adjust and find fish elsewhere. You didn't go through the work to find them. If you don't take the time to understand the movement of bass in a particular lake, you're done. Getting local help doesn't help you learn a lake like you need to for tournament-level success."

While Scalish doesn't rely on local angler information in general, he notes that some local tournament anglers are going to be very knowledgeable about a lake. "They know the lake inside and out. Those guys can give you incredible information. There are a lot of guys on tour who are able to get good local information, and you can win tournaments on this information. Here's the deal: Unless you know these guys personally, they are not going to give you their ace in the hole [place to fish]." He points out that local anglers might give their D+ or C fishing spots, but generally not their A+ spots.

"Local information could destroy you when you fish higher-level tournaments," adds Scalish. In his first Elite BASS tournament, he listened to a competitor who was also a friend. Scalish had what he thought was a good practice session, but his friend mentioned that he was "killing" them on a certain pattern. So, thinking he needed to get better-quality fish to win the tournament, Scalish decided to change his fishing pattern. It turned out that had he stuck to his original pattern, he more than likely would have placed better than seventh in that tournament.

Scalish points out that having a trusted small group of people to bounce fishing

■ **Frank Scalish pulled this "quality" fish from the lily pads using a Texas-rigged YUM Lizard.** LURENET.COM

ideas off of is very important. You need a way to vent and clear your head before the tournament, but too many ideas and options can be fatal to your chances of success. "My best tournaments are the ones where I don't have preconceived notions. I let the fish dictate to me what I have to do. In a tournament on Lake Erie, I came back from eighty-ninth place to finish fourth. That's because I didn't lock myself into a pattern or certain ideas. Years ago on another Jerry Rind tournament on Kerr Reservoir, my partner and I were catching big 5-pound-plus fish on

secondary points. We thought we were going to win the tournament—we were catching 20-plus pounds of fish without even trying. Then we fished the tournament and came in with two fish. What happened? The water level on the lake came up a foot. The fish went to the back of the pockets and got into the wood. The guys that were flipping, they killed us. It was like we weren't even on the same lake! You can't lock yourself into a pattern."

Scroggins: "You meet different people from around the various regions, and it helps if you know somebody. This is a catch-22. When I first started, I always wanted to talk to them [local anglers]. Today, I don't do that nearly as much. Here's what happens: Instead of going out and finding your own fish, someone tells you where they are. Now you have to go and look at that instead of doing your own thing. If the fish are not there, then you still have to find your own fish. So, you lose a lot of your time. It's better to go out and do your own thing."

Mason: "Very seldom do local anglers win on their home body of water. A lot of times the pros will come in and find an area that locals don't fish and do very well off of it. I would say that when I go to a lake, maybe a quarter of what I fish will be based on what a local angler might tell me. These are people I know and have a relationship with. If I ask a local, it's someone I trust.

"Over time you'll meet local anglers in and around a body of water who you'll get to know and trust. Whether it's a relative, a good friend, or a co-angler you've met at another tournament, you'll establish a local network of people who can help you in your pretournament research."

Overall, Mason considers local angler resources "a double-edged sword, something you have to be really careful with. Occasionally, I will get local information. Most of the time, I don't live and die by it." If he uses local information at all, he's looking for histories of different parts of the lake or river, such as specific colors that seem to work better than others on a specific area or segment of the water.

"Some of my best friends have been co-anglers I've met over the years. At the same time, you don't want to base all you do on what locals tell you. It's very easy for locals to develop blind spots on a lake. That's why many times tournaments are won on a spot that locals don't consider to be one of the really choice fishing locations."

Howell: While very wary of local angler advice, Howell takes a "networking" approach to developing relationships. He emphasizes that over time you should try to make contact with as many people as possible in the area of the lake or river so you can begin to develop a good networking list: "Now, fifteen years later, I've got a book that's too big to even carry with me that's full of names and cards. I've got two or three people in every state who know something about anywhere I'm going to go fishing now, so I don't have to just blindly call people anymore."

Taking Notes

Keeping records on key areas to fish and noting the effects of seasonal and weather patterns on the bass is crucial to becoming a winning tournament professional. Whether you mark spots with your GPS on electronic maps, make notes on a paper map, jot observations down in a notebook, or talk into a digital tape recorder, keeping a record of your fishing experiences on a body of water is critical to success. Compiling data and organizing

■ Some pros use small digital recorders like this one to record detailed notes during practice for review later. DAVID DIRKS

it helps you become a highly effective competitor.

Scalish: "Any structure I find in a lake gets labeled on my GPS. Now I let my GPS harbor the information. I always carry my maps with me and mark them."

Mason: "From a preparation standpoint, there are no secrets. It's about being prepared and well-versed on what the lake is like and on the tournament conditions in the past. I'll make notes in a notebook that I carry with me, then when I get home I organize my thoughts in a more defined way. I'll take just general

notes while I'm there on the water during practice."

By the time he gets to a lake, Mason has from ten to twenty pages of handwritten notes and several maps. "I create a file folder or binder for every lake that I'm going to fish during the year. In addition to the notes, I'll have a summary page that outlines what I want to do on the lake and how to do it. How do I want to start on my first day of practice? I'll include a list of specific baits I'll need to bring with me. I have my Navionics chip and the spots marked that I think should fit the pattern for the season I'm fishing." On his Lowrance system, Mason marks the areas he noted in his pretournament study in bright blue and the fishing spots he located during practice in bright red so he can look at his screen and immediately know how each spot was found.

Swett: In addition to his written notes, Swett always carries a digital camera with him and takes pictures of specific spots that he wants to note for the current tournament as well as future ones. "If you do this, you need to keep a log of each shot, noting the specific location in relation to the lake map. This will help you to easily relate the photo to a specific area on the lake."

Howell: "I have files for each lake that are labeled for the current year. I'll add an after-tournament summary on what I should have done, what weight won the tournament, and what pattern was predominant." Over time, Howell has accumulated thick files that are rich with information that helps him to plan his fishing in any season and under any conditions. "If you fish a certain body of water long enough, you begin to learn how to fish it in all kinds of weather conditions."

The Limitations of Pretournament Research

Pretournament research, no matter how extensively done, is never foolproof.

Top professional anglers make it a point to never get too hung up on what their research is telling them. Research can help you narrow down the areas you want to check out first, depending upon seasonality, but it's never a replacement for actually just fishing.

Scalish: "I was fishing a tournament at Clear Lake in California, which I had never fished before. I researched the lake on the Internet and found out that there are some giant fish in this lake. Generally, 17 to 18 pounds of fish a day is in the money. What I didn't know until I got there was that they had sprayed the lake and had killed off most of the vegetation. Where there used to be miles and miles of vegetation that went hundreds of yards offshore, there was now little tiny, skinny strands of vegetation along the bank. What that did was make all those fish that were coming shallow to spawn more accessible. Instead of being in the thick vegetation, where they could spread out and have gobs of cover, they now were totally accessible and easy to catch, which I didn't know. I had about 18 pounds of fish a day and ended up in seventy-second place. Here I had thought I was going to get a check with no problem, but my [daily] weights weren't even close. These giant fish were roaming around, and everyone throwing swim baits was coming in contact with these huge 10-pounders."

CHAPTER TWO

Pretournament Preparation

If you've participated in or witnessed enough tournaments, you've undoubtedly seen this story unfold: A tournament angler is methodically working the water with his bait. After many successive casts, he feels the strike and pulls to set the hook. He can feel it—it's a big, heavy fish. It's a tournament-winning fish or, at the very least, a check-generating fish. The battle unfolds, with the bass doing its best to break off and the angler doing his best to bring it to the boat. Then, as suddenly as it began, the fight ends. No bass, no bait—it's gone. The angler drops to his knees, and his contorted face says it all. He knows something went wrong, and he's just put the win and the check out of reach.

What went wrong? It could have been any number of things, but most likely his line was frayed at some point near his bait. It might have had a nick in it, causing it to break off. Or maybe a nick in the top rod guide managed to chew on the line, making it weak.

Whatever it was, the angler knows he should have checked everything. But there wasn't enough time, he says to himself. Not enough time for careful pretournament inspection of his equipment? It's a tough lesson to learn.

Most of us are used to seeing the glamour and the excitement of the tournament weigh-ins. On both the local and national levels, days of practice and tournament play lead up to the "big event." What you don't see, but is absolutely necessary for a tournament angler to either win or just take home a check, is the preparation before it all begins. You don't see the hours and hours spent by pros like Terry Scroggins, making sure everything—including terminal tackle, baits, boats, and trucks—are in top running condition. It's not glamorous and it's probably not much fun, but it's the work of the successful tournament bass angler.

After your pretournament research, gathering the right terminal tackle and checking its performance, sorting and organizing the baits you deem necessary for a win, and making sure that your boat and truck are ready are critical to your success.

Preparing for a Tournament

Paul Elias spends about two full days before each tournament getting his terminal tackle

Frank Scalish gets another rod ready for practice time.
LURENET.COM

and other gear ready for fishing. "I'll take all the rods and reels out of the boat. I'll line them up and decide which ones I'm going to need for the lake. Am I going to need three flipping sticks and three cranking rods? Two spinnerbait rods and two jig rods? Once I decide on which ones I'm taking, I strip them all of line and put new line on them. Most of my time is spent going through all the tackle in my boat, trying to eliminate stuff I know I'm not going to use. I'll take two plastic containers with things I won't put in the boat but I might need during the tournament." Elias generally carries eighteen to twenty rods on the boat in any given tournament. In most general fishing situations, he has at least three spinning rods, with the balance being baitcasting rods.

For practice time, Elias generally will whittle his lure selection down as much as possible: "For instance, I may have four tackle boxes with jerkbaits. I will take all those with me to the tournament but only have one box in my boat. I try to take a good variety of those jerkbaits, then I'll decide after practice if I need to subtract from or add to my boat. I'll do that with every version of lure I have."

Terry Scroggins: "When I prepare my boat for a practice day, I like to have twenty-five or thirty rods rigged with whatever kinds of bait you could imagine. That's what practice is—to learn what they are going to bite or not bite. After three days of practice, I like to narrow it down to about ten rods. It's just a process of

elimination as to what the fish are going to bite. The drop-shot, shaky-head worm is huge across the country. That's a bait that can catch you a limit and probably cash a check for you but more than likely is not going to win the event. But you have to have one of those [finesse rods] in your arsenal just for backup. I'm more of a power fisherman than anything. I like to throw crankbaits, flip heavy cover, throw a spinnerbait, and just cover a lot of water. I like to go to those types of baits, but at the same time, I'm not scared to fall back on a shaky-head or drop-shot to catch a few fish."

Sam Swett: Swett refers to the process of getting his fishing tackle ready as "getting my gear tuned to the lake." This means making sure that the line and the rods and reels match the water he will be fishing and his basic practice strategy. "When I'm doing my pretournament research, I'm making mental notes about the baits that I need to bring. When I do that, I jot them down on a list. I have about eight large containers which I start loading up with baits. Inevitably, while I'm at a tournament, there will be something that they're biting on that I don't have with me but have at home. I don't take everything, but I try to take as much as I can in anticipation of what I'll need." By the time practice comes, he's ready to start whittling down some of those baits to the ones he'll definitely need during the tournament.

Swett prefers to prepare his boat by getting to the tournament a day before

■ These rods are rigged and ready to go in preparation for a tournament. LURENET.COM

practice begins. "I literally pull out all the rods I have and go through my tackle. All my tackle boxes will be organized for that particular tournament." He likens the process to a mechanic who pulls out the tools he'll need to work on a specific part of a vehicle.

Swett also makes sure that he adds fresh line to all his reels. He keeps a variety of line sizes on his reels to insure he's prepared to fish whatever water conditions he finds at the tournaments. He recommends carrying 6- to 20-pound-test lines of both monofilament and fluorocarbon in 2-pound increments. "Don't let price stand in your way of buying larger spools of line. A lot of people don't respool their lines during a tournament. There are so many bad things that can happen to your line underneath the water. It's very important to keep your reels spooled with fresh line."

He recommends buying the larger spools of line, like 2,500- or 3,000-yard spools. "With smaller line spools, there is so much line waste. On smaller spools, you generally don't have enough to spool more than one reel, so buying the larger spools is more efficient and sometimes less expensive."

Swett has around thirty-six rods/reels that he brings to every tournament. "I try to keep at least a half dozen as flipping sticks and another half dozen as spinning reels for drop-shots, or shaky-head worm fishing, or any finesse-type fishing. I'll have another seven or eight spinnerbait rods that are rigged for everything from an

eighth ounce to an ounce or ounce and a quarter. You want enough rods on hand to match the conditions. Some rods are multipurpose rods. For instance, my Carolina-rigged rods are very efficient for frogging. If I'm throwing a YUM Buzz Frog, for example, I know I can throw a Carolina rig with the same rod."

"I'm always checking my drag," says Swett, "to make sure nothing sticks on my drag during practice or the tournament. On my rods, I'll take a Q-tip and run it through each guide to make sure I'm not getting any line frayed or anything that could damage the line. I'll look for splintering on the rod because I don't want to set the hook on a fish and have the rod splinter on me." Swett also carefully checks each reel to insure the ball bearings are still smooth.

Frank Scalish: "Rods are easy to maintain. I use Lemon Pledge on all my rods. The wax coating helps keep grime and gunk from sticking on your rod. Also, it slicks up the guides so they cast smoother. I'll clean the rods with a damp paper towel and then rub them down with Lemon Pledge. If a rod handle gets dirty and grimy, I use 900-grade sandpaper on it. It won't take a lot of cork off, but it will take the dirt off.

"I check the level line gear to make sure there is no grass on it. I take a Q-tip and clean the line guide. For the most part, if I have been fishing brackish water [mix of fresh and salt water], I take the reels apart and clean them." Outside of

▮ **Rigging rods is a labor of love for Sam Swett. He, like other pros, spends hours before each tournament doing it.** SAM SWETT

fishing brackish water or not performing well, Scalish will break down his reels and clean and lube them once per season. "If you start hearing sounds or the reel is not performing well, then take it apart."

Scalish, like many tournament pros, spends a lot of time organizing his baits. He has containers for individual types of bait and keeps a reasonable amount of each on his boat. As he uses up baits during practices and tournaments, he'll replenish them with inventory stored in containers in his truck. When he returns

from a tournament, he'll replenish the truck inventory with the inventory kept in his basement. This way, his boat and truck inventory are always replenished and full.

"I see guys, especially nonboaters, who will waste more time looking for stuff than I could ever imagine wasting in a day. Having an unorganized system wastes enough time in the day to literally cost you a limit. I know people who throw all their soft plastics in a container. When they are fishing, they'll open the container and start hunting through it. By the end of the day,

■ The time to organize your baits is well before you're on the road for a tournament. DAVID DIRKS

that could cost you a half hour [of tournament time]."

A Word on Buying Tackle

There is a lot of debate over what quality of tackle you should consider acquiring for tournament fishing. The bass tackle business is a multibillion-dollar industry in the United States alone. Unlike a few decades ago, the variety of terminal tackle, baits, and lines available to bass anglers is huge and sometimes overwhelming. While you'll hardly find uniform agreement on what

types of tackle to buy, almost all tournament anglers agree on this: Buying tackle of any kind is driven by personal preference. It's what works for you that counts. It has nothing to do with how much you can spend either—it's a matter of which rod or reel feels best in your hand. This is a completely personal experience. Nonetheless, there are a few points to consider that will help you make your way through the bewildering array of modern tackle.

Swett: "The thing about fishing gear is confidence. You don't need $500 or $1,000 rod/reel combinations. They are nice and they will last the distance, and you do get what you pay for. But you'll always have the person who will pick up a $50 rod and shake it and feel it. They might like that rod. Another person can pick up the same rod and say, 'It's too flimsy' or 'It's not what I need.' A lot of it is personal preference.

"I try not to let price put a limit on me. I want to be sure I have the right equipment and the right sensitivity to do what I need to do." He emphasizes finding that combination of rod and reel that you are not only comfortable with, but also helps you stay sensitive to the fish. Your fishing equipment has to fit like a glove that is molded to your hand perfectly. For Swett, a rod is nothing more than an extension of his arm. It has to be able to allow him to feel underwater stumps, across grass or gravel, or a strike. It has to transmit what's happening under the water to him.

"Use the same reel if possible, other than changing for reel speed [ratio]. When I'm casting or retrieving, I palm the reel a lot. I want to have that same feel in my hand. I want paddles of the handle to be the same. When I lay one rod down and pick up another, I feel like I didn't make a transition [with the rod]. Although the action of the rod might change, it feels just like the last one."

Elias: "It all depends on a person's financial situation. Some people feel like they have to have the best of everything. I think with the product lines that most of these companies have today, you can find a very good rig in the middle class of the line they have. As you progress and you get better [at tournament fishing], there are features on rods and reels that you may want."

Scalish: "You are either going to have good equipment or not. Better equipment is going to translate into better feel, sensitivity, and casting capabilities. You have to pick out the best possible equipment you can afford in both rods and reels. It's going to last you longer, which makes it cheaper in the long run." Scalish points out that the critical factor of fishing better should not be underestimated: "A ten-ball-bearing reel is going to work better than a four-ball-bearing reel."

As proof of this point, Scalish has ten-ball-bearing reels that are fifteen years old that he's still using today. "Rods and reels are nothing to skimp on. I'm not saying you have to go out and buy a $350 reel, because I don't own a $350 reel. The reality is that you want to look for reels that have multiple ball bearings and good-quality construction."

Scalish prefers to fish his Powell rods at 7 feet 3 inches. He also uses the exact same brand and style of reels every time. "Every time I pick up a rod, it feels exactly the same. There's no difference. I know guys who fish with different rods and reels, but I think at that point, you're not giving yourself an advantage."

Randy Howell: Early in his career, Howell was amazed to learn how better gear helped to improve his fishing, noting "The better you fish and the better you cast, the more your confidence level goes up." If you don't have a lot of money to spend, he believes it's much better to have one very high-quality outfit than to have three cheaper ones.

Howell divides his rods into three key groups: heavy action, medium action, and spinning rods. The stiff heavy-action rods are for power, for setting the hook on set-ups like Carolina rigs, jigs, flipping, and pitching. Medium-action 61/2- to 7-foot rods are used for spinnerbaits, jerkbaits, and topwater baits. He feels that medium- or medium/heavy-action rods in those sizes are good all-around rods to have. Howell rounds out his choices by emphasizing that you need to have spinning rods. He prefers 6-foot-10-inch or 7-foot medium- to medium/heavy-action spinning rods.

More about Fishing Lines

Taking care of line is critical. Store your line in an area that will not subject it to extreme heat. Heat deteriorates the quality and strength of a line. It doesn't take much to nick line, and you're probably not going to see the nick until it's way too late. Is it worth losing a fish that could help you win a tournament? Ask anyone who has lost a fish because of a nick in the line, and you might see tears well up in their eyes.

Swett: "I keep my fishing line in an ice cooler. That way, if there is a major change in conditions, it's not going to affect the line." In either extreme heat or cold, an insulated cooler will help moderate the air temperature affecting the line. "Your fishing line is your life line—it's what puts fish in the boat. So you want to take care of your fishing line." After a tournament, don't leave your fishing line on the boat or in the basement. Bring it in to where you can keep it in a 65- to 85-degree air temperature area.

Making sure you have a variety of line sizes is critical, according to Swett. "I use different lines for different applications. I make sure I pack the amount and variety of line I need. If I'm going to predominately do finesse fishing, I bring enough small-diameter line. If I'm going to be frog fishing or fishing super-heavy cover, I bring plenty of braided line. If I'm throwing topwater, then I also bring plenty of monofilament line. For bottom fishing, like with a Carolina rig or tube fishing, I'll have plenty of fluorocarbon."

For topwater fishing, monofilament is the way to go, primarily because it floats. When fishing topwater lures like a Pop'R or Zara Spook, Swett sometimes uses a thicker-diameter monofilament line. "Some people will tell me, 'I can't get the topwater action of my bait to work properly.' That's because they are sometimes using 20-pound fluorocarbon line [that sinks]."

Scalish: "I use braided lines for Carolina-rigging, throwing Super Spooks, and for throwing rattle baits. For Carolina-rigging, braided line is my main line with a monofilament leader." Scalish uses a monofilament line leader for this setup primarily because monofilament, as opposed

■ Applying a line conditioner before a tournament keeps your line and reel in good working order. DAVID DIRKS

to fluorocarbon leader, floats and keeps his rig off the bottom better. Given that braided lines have little or no stretch, Scalish prefers the extra sensitivity you get by using braid for a Carolina rig.

"For my flipping, drop-shot, and Texas-rigged worms, or any soft plastic presentation, I'm using fluorocarbon exclusively. Fluorocarbon offers less stretch, better sensitivity, and better hookups [than using monofilament]. For crankbaits, spinnerbaits, and jerkbaits, I use Silver Thread, which is a monofilament. The only time I'll change to fluorocarbon with my crankbaits and jerkbaits is if I want to get them down deeper. The characteristics of fluorocarbon will help me gain a little more depth. Monofilament will also keep your suspending jerkbaits suspended."

Howell: "I was a light-line man in my early years [on the tour] for sight fishing. As I got into areas that were rougher and tougher with brush, trees, and a lot of cover, I started using bigger, heavier tackle. As I did that, I started realizing that the fish never seemed to be too sensitive about my [heavier] line. It was more about how I presented the bait, how I read the fish, and how I moved [the bait] and did things at the right times. When you're fishing against the clock, if you can cut down on the time it takes to catch one, the faster you can go after another one."

Howell will generally use a 30-pound Spiderwire Stealth braid for his startup presentations. He'll match the line with a 7-foot medium/heavy-action baitcasting rod with a fast-retrieve reel, because when every second counts, you want to be able to pull the bait back to the boat and then get it back out there as fast as you can.

Checking Your Bass Boat

Not unlike race car drivers who depend totally on the operating performance of their vehicles, tournament anglers need their boats to be in top shape prior to a tournament. Having a mechanical breakdown during a tournament means the loss of precious time that could have been spent catching a quality limit of fish. Fortunately, most problems are clearly preventable or can be taken care of well before the tournament starts.

Swett: Swett does all his boat checking and maintenance at least a week before a tournament and the day before he leaves for practice, just to make sure everything is in top performance shape. This kind of maintenance discipline gives him plenty of time to fix any problems that come up well before the tournament starts.

"Inspect the batteries, checking for any corrosion. Make sure that they are fully charged each day of both practice and tournament time. Turn on your aerators and bilge pump to make sure they are working properly. Also check the electrical connection on both the aerator and the bilge pump, making sure there is no corrosion buildup. Check all the circuit breaker terminals for corrosion.

■ Checking battery connections is something no pro skips. Like most pros, Terry Scroggins checks his every day. DAVID DIRKS

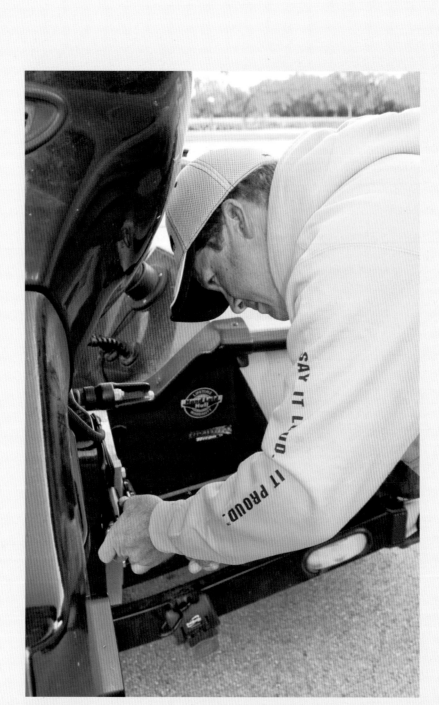

■ Scroggins carefully checks his engine and the mounts that hold it in place as part of his pretournament preparation. DAVID DIRKS

"Check all the running lights. Make sure the engine fires up on the first try, and check that the kill switch is working well too. Run all the GPS and other electronics."

As for the appearance of your boat, Swett says, "If you're going to try to obtain sponsors or already have sponsors, it is crucial to have a clean boat and equipment." Nothing says professionalism louder than equipment that is always clean and presentable in public.

Scroggins: "In cold weather, like anything less than 40 degrees, you really need to let your engine warm up before you use it for a good five to ten minutes. I actually blew an engine up one time. It was 18 degrees and I didn't let it warm up as long as I should have. I made it about a mile down the river and blew the engine."

Scalish: Scalish recommends checking the motor and jackplate bolts and making sure they are tight. He always checks everything that holds the motor to the boat and the jackplate. "These boats take a beating, and the bolts will loosen up on the jackplate or loosen up on the transom."

Organizing Your Bass Boat

Almost all pros have their own personal way

▥ **Having your rods and favorite baits ready for action is critical. Note how this rod is labeled with a 12 to indicate what pound test line is on the reel.** SAM SWETT

BOAT ITEMS CHECKLIST

Have a special "boat kit" on board that contains tools and other items to help you keep your boat in top running condition or make a quick repair while on the water. Here's a list of some of the items typically in this kit.

- Superglue
- Electrical tape
- Spare washers
- Bolts
- Nuts
- Crescent wrench
- Pair of wire cutters
- Channel lock
- Prop wrenches

- Phillips and flat-head screwdrivers
- Duct tape
- Pair of very sharp scissors
- Pliers
- Set of ruby sharpening stones
- Zap-A-Gap (for securing knots)
- Allen keys
- Socket wrench set
- Electrician's tape

■ **Basic pro tools: wire cutters and an all-purpose tool.** DAVID DIRKS

- Cordless drill (to tighten screws without having to do it by hand and eat into your practice or tournament time)

- Black, brown, olive, and red Sharpie markers (for modifying color shades on baits)

- Sunscreen, extra sunglasses, and rain jacket

- (Don't depend on your fishing partner to bring his or her own Life jacket. Always have an extra one.)

- Buy good-quality tools that can hold up to the abuse of moisture, and keep them in a watertight box.

of organizing their boat and the tackle that goes with it for tournament fishing. But for all their differences, they all agree that an organized boat allows you to fish more efficiently and effectively. Efficiency is about doing things right, and effectiveness is about doing the right things. You'll develop your own organizing style, but your goal will be the same as your nearby competitor: keeping your gear organized so that you can quickly switch tackle, baits, and techniques quickly. This enables you to spend more time fishing than wasting valuable tournament time trying to locate what you need.

Scalish: "I'm tackle heavy in my boat. I carry a lot of stuff for about every scenario you could imagine. But, it's all labeled and it's all in small plastic boxes. It's too much trouble for me to go to a tournament, unload my boat, and put in just what I need for that tournament, then have to pack up and go to my next tournament and reload the boat. I don't do that."

Scalish says that as long as your tackle and baits are well-organized on the boat and you can get to them easily, there's no reason not to load your boat up with as much as it can safely hold.

Scroggins: "You want to be careful how you load your boat. You want to have all your heavy stuff toward the back of the boat, like your plastic worms and hardbaits. I like to have everything I'm going to use in the front of the boat so I don't have to take more than a step to get to it. At the same time, you don't want a lot of heavy weight in the front of the boat. What that does is make the front of the boat heavy to where you can't make it lift. You need to get the nose of the boat out of the water to run fast. If you're on a long run and you have a lot of weight in the boat, you can actually lose 4 to 5 miles per hour, which is critical in a tournament.

"I might also have twenty-five tackle boxes with me in the truck and boat. When it comes down to the tournament, I like to just get down to no more than seven or eight boxes in the boat. Have those labeled so you can grab what you need."

Scroggins likes to have all his crank-bait rods packed on one side of the boat and his worm- and jig-fishing rods on the other.

For Swett, the organization of his boat is based on his plan for how he will approach his practice time. Most often, he'll bring more gear and baits during practice and use that time to determine what gear he won't need to bring during the tournament. As the practice progresses, Swett repacks his boat each day, adding or removing tackle and baits as necessary: "I let the practice day tell me what gear I'll need for the next day and reload my boat accordingly."

Swett suggests developing a routine for packing your tackle into both your boat and towing vehicle. The more you get into a routine for organizing and packing, the more sensitive you'll be to whether you're missing something before you hit the road. "You have to find what works for you."

Mental Preparation

Most competitive anglers understand that

■ Keeping your boat organized during practice time makes for less work when tournament time comes around. DAVID DIRKS

some anxiety just before a tournament is a natural occurrence. Sometimes it's more or less about how much confidence you have in your abilities to fish a particular lake. High confidence levels can reduce anxiety and help you mentally prepare for the tournament. Reduced anxiety means that you'll fish more effectively and be able to make clearer decisions. As we will see in future chapters, it's decision-making that separates the winners from the losers.

Swett: "After seventeen years of tournament fishing, I still get butterflies in my stomach at takeoff time in the morning [of a tournament]. It's a make or break time, and the tournament is getting ready to start. One thing I learned, and I learned it from my dad, is that I've got to have fun. The more fun I have fishing, the more my natural ability comes back out. Then I can rely on myself to catch fish and not be intimidated by everyone else."

Scalish does two things when he finds himself anxious either before or during a tournament: 1) He finds a good comedy movie and watches it. He says it helps him forget about the anxiety before a tournament—he just laughs it off. 2) If he's having a tough time, he'll work to bring his positive mental attitude back by remembering all the tournaments he's won and the high points of his career. In competitive angling, having high levels of anxiety or self-doubt will not help you win a tournament or even place in a money spot.

"It's easy to [mentally] unravel," says Scalish. "And the bigger the [tournament] stakes, the easier it is to unravel. You can't do that because it'll affect your judgment on the water."

CHAPTER THREE

Pretournament Practice

Practice time for a tournament bass angler is one of the most critical points in the buildup to the "big day." Well before the cameras begin rolling or the fans start to show up, the professional angler is putting his boat in the water. It's a time for figuring out the fish: What are they doing now? Where are they? What will it take to get them to bite? Where are the "limit" fish? Where are the "quality" fish? Do I have the right tackle prepared? What am I missing? What part of the lake or river is "hot"? How many quality spots can I find before the tournament begins? Where do I start?

These questions, and the many more that follow, will lead to a tournament victory if answered correctly. During practice time, all of your competitors will try to answer the same questions. So while all competitors may start on a level playing field, once practice time begins, the field begins to get uneven. Those who know how to use their practice time effectively will find themselves fishing and winning more consistently.

Effective Practice Time

Terry Scroggins: "What I'll do in practice is find four or five areas in three days where I think I can catch them [fish] pretty good. I'll start on those spots and try to catch five good ones. And then I'll expand on that and keep practicing throughout the tournament, trying to find new locations where I can catch another limit the next day." To Scroggins, it's the never-ending practice time. And it's a winning strategy that helps keep him in the top of most of the tournaments he fishes. "You have to be open-minded and not afraid to fish new water during the tournament. In other words, when the tournament starts, my practice is not over—I keep practicing."

For fishing a body of water you're not so familiar with, Scroggins recommends limiting yourself to a 10-mile area and learning that area very well before you go to other parts of the lake. "A big body of water can overwhelm you. You go there and say, 'Wow, how am I going to cover this?' Before you know it, you're trying to cover all of it. It'll end up messing you up instead of helping you."

Scroggins divides a lake into three sections and fishes the farthest section from the boat ramp on practice day one. On the second day of practice, he'll hit the middle third of that distance, and on the last day of practice, he fishes the area closest to the launch ramp. This not only gives him a chance to cover a lot of water, but it also has a practical side: getting him to the tournament briefing on time. Most tournaments conduct mandatory briefings on the last day of practice.

As for specific places to concentrate on, Scroggins offers this advice: "If I go to a lake that I don't know anything about, the number one thing I'll do is fish all the boat ramps and all the marinas. That's where all the fish get turned loose [after tournaments]. Keep in mind that they have club tournaments and local boat tournaments [during the year]. A big population of fish gets turned loose in those places." It's a good place to start when you haven't fished a body of water that much.

"What I do in practice is try to find two or three spots a day. Over three days of practice, you've got at least six spots. If you have six spots going into a tournament, that's a very productive practice. On the first day of the tournament, I'll fish those six spots and catch what I can catch. As I'm moving around, I'm still looking for new water." Scroggins uses his tournament

time as additional "practice" time as well. He's always on the lookout for more good-producing spots to fish. It helps him set up his plan of attack for each tournament day. Scroggins doesn't worry about what he'll do at the beginning of each day, since he's already done his homework the day before.

He also pays a lot of attention to the contours and geographic layout of the lake: "If it has high banks and a lot of hills around it, you can normally fish tighter to the bank. If it's a low-lying lake, a flatter lake, then I like to fish more offshore."

To gain more confidence during your practice time, Scroggins recommends starting off with light-line tackle, like a shaky-head drop-shot, and catching numbers of fish. "Even though it's a small fish bait, I've caught a lot of 7- to 8-pound fish on a shaky-head worm. That will generate more bites and give you more confidence in an area. Then you can come back with a crankbait or spinnerbait and try to catch a bigger fish. You've got to know they live there before you can catch them."

As for the use of electronics during practice, Scroggins says, "You've got to trust your electronics 100 percent. If it says there are fish down there, you've got to believe it and make them bite. If you start doubting your equipment, you're in trouble."

Scroggins believes it's critical, despite your experience and history with a particular body of water, to fish in the

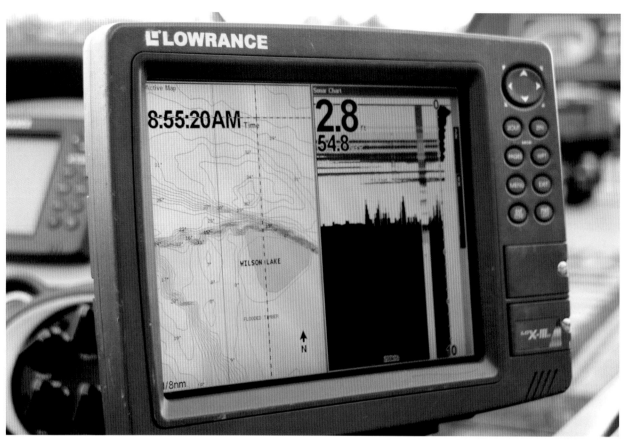

■ Checking your boat electronics system every day during both practice and tournament time will help you build confidence in it. DAVID DIRKS

present and not in the past. "You can also get in trouble by knowing too much. It doesn't matter if you're fishing at home or 2,000 miles away from home—you have to fish in the moment. You have to fish to what's going on in the present time.

"In practice you might have found fish tight to cover or on a ledge—the sun is up high, and there are slick water conditions with a little bit of current moving. On the first day of the tournament, it's now cloudy, windy, with no current moving. They are not going to be where you found them during practice. They might be 100 yards

away doing something different." This is another example of why it's critical to keep an open mind and be prepared for changing conditions.

Jimmy Mason: "A lot depends on how much practice time you have and how much experience you have on any given body of water. In the Elite Series, we have basically two and a half days of practice. A lot of the lakes, especially in the first couple of years [on the tour], most anglers have never been to. In those situations, the best thing to do is pick one section of the lake—be it one creek or one 10-mile section [of lake]—and spend the first two days really learning it. If the first day [of practice] goes well, then I will spend the second day in the same general area trying to refine the pattern more. I'm trying to find more areas close by that match the pattern." Mason ties that in with the local long-range weather forecast for the tournament. Things like cold fronts and drops or rises in water levels can play a major role as to what the fish will do.

On a lake Mason has never fished, he spends the first day just learning the lake—riding around it, never making a cast. "I'll look at all the areas that caught my eye during the pretournament preparation. What's the water color? Is there more or less cover than I thought it was going to be?" He's also looking for bait, paying close attention to his electronics to see if the bait is at a higher or lower depth in the water. Mason is disciplined and takes handwritten notes during each practice day. He sometimes even uses a digital recorder to document what he's learning about the lake.

If he decides to fish another section of the lake based on the results from his first practice day, he'll compare the two practice days. Which practice area provided the better results? On his third day of practice, he'll focus his attention on the area that shows the greatest promise of fishing results.

How do you prioritize which spots you start with on day one of the tournament? "Everyone at the Elite Series is a heck of a fisherman," Mason says. "Everybody is very good mechanically. What separates who wins and who finishes badly is strictly based on decision-making. Every spot you go to is a calculated risk."

Randy Howell: Based on his research, Howell will generally pick a few areas that match the type of seasonal fishing expected for that lake. If the fish are shallow, for example, he'll look for the most promising shallow areas. Once he arrives on the lake for practice, his priority is getting to those areas and exploring them. "I'm looking at my Lowrance electronics, figuring out the contour of the area. Then I'll start fishing. If I start catching some, I then start figuring out if there is a pattern here. The first day [of practice] is all about the areas I researched." Howell's initial plan either helps him find productive water or helps him eliminate water.

On his second day of practice, he is applying what he has learned from day one to start his day of fishing. "I'm more of a natural instinct, intuitive fisherman. I learn more by riding around [the water] and looking. That's not something you learn by reading books or watching videos. You get that only by spending time on the water."

As Howell travels the country doing fishing seminars, he often hears that one of the biggest mistakes many weekend, local, and regional tournament anglers make is overfishing an area. Overfishing just leads to inconsistent results. You might catch multiple fish in one area one day, but then come back the following day and catch

■ **You'll find hundreds of books available on basic bass fishing today. Tour pros recommend a constant learning program.** DAVID DIRKS

next to nothing. "When I practice and go into an area and start fishing, if I'm fishing a bait that's a reaction bait like a crankbait or Rat-L-Trap, I'll keep my hooks on the bait to start with." After he catches a fish or two in an area, Howell knows enough to stop fishing that area and start fishing another. He also knows that if he was able to catch a few fish there, there are probably more in the area. It generally doesn't pay to disturb all the fish by catching them during practice time.

To reduce catches during practices, Howell will clip the barbs off his lure,

leaving just enough bend in the hook to allow him to feel a fish but not catch it. This is a common tactic in tournament circles.

To find out what the fish are keying on for food, Howell will examine a fish's mouth to see if there is any baitfish or crawfish in it. Sometimes, it's paying attention to those little things that can help you determine what the fish want. "Seeing is believing," says Howell.

Paul Elias: "I usually pick an area of the lake that's been producing [fish]." For example, Elias might find out that most of

■ Paul Elias displays two excellent examples of tournament "quality" fish. LURENET.COM

the fish are being taken from up the river channel and that there are several creeks connected to the river. He will then go and concentrate on as many creeks as possible during one practice day. If he finds those areas producing well, he might decide to spend most of his practice time exploring the river and its feeder creeks. He will also try to find something close to the weigh-in area.

"I feel if I find one good area a day in practice, I'm doing well. That gives me three areas in the tournament. If it's a hard tournament and you've only found one place to get good bites in, you go there and stay. You try to get as good a stringer as you can pick out. There are times after the practice period that you realize that you didn't really accomplish a strategy to win the tournament. You need to survive this tournament, try to get a check, and go on to the next one."

Elias has never been one to try to cover the whole lake. "I've always picked an area of a lake that I thought I would like to fish. I would really work on that area. I very seldom run a real long way [from the boat launch]. I try to put something together within a reasonable distance from the takeoff."

If he knows it's going to take a lot of fish to win a particular tournament, he feels he needs to have at least ten to fifteen bites a day in practice in order to feel that he's going to do well. "If I go to a lake that I know that 10 to 12 pounds a day is solid [for a win] and there is an abundance of

fish, that's a practice time that really needs to be watched closely. What happens on those types of lakes is that [anglers] are sticking a lot of fish in the practice period because they are trying to find the better-sized fish. I found that if most of the fish are averaging 1.5 pounds and every now and then you catch a 4-pounder, if you've caught that 4-pounder, you've really hurt yourself.

"You've got to be both lucky and good. You're not going to eliminate the luck factor on those 4- to 6-pounders when everyone else is catching 2-pounders. But, there is a difference between luck and setting a pattern that's giving you 15 pounds [of fish] a day in a 10- to 12-pound-average tournament. That's not luck, that's skill."

Two things Elias always studies during practice time are the baitfish and water temperature. "I'm always looking for the baitfish. They [the bass] are going to be near the baitfish. Now, it may not be schools of shad. It may be an obvious thing that bluegills are hanging around. Sometimes you'll see a lot of bluegills around the bank or hanging around a dock. Bass eat bluegills, so there'll be some bass around.

"The other major thing is water temperature, especially in the spring and fall. If you can find an area on the lake in the early spring or late fall that might be a little warmer and there is a good mixture of baitfish in there, you're probably going to catch some fish."

Elias also pays close attention to his electronics during practice. "A bass fisherman is always looking at his electronics. I don't care if he's in 2 feet of water. There's always that time when all of a sudden you see something on your depth finder. It might have gone from 2 feet [in depth] to 3.5 feet. A little break like that in shallow water can be just like a creek ledge in 12 to 20 feet of water. So those are the kinds of things you need to be constantly monitoring for and deciding whether it's worth looking at. The depth finders are so sophisticated now that they can draw a stump out [on the monitor]. If you're fishing a lake that doesn't have a lot of cover and you're watching your depth finder in 5 feet of water and it draws a stump out, that's something I'm going to want to check out. I'm going to circle around and fish that stump." It only takes a few seconds to miss some structure or cover that you just drove over.

When fishing a lake that receives heavy pressure from the great number of tournaments hosted on it, Elias will try a different tactic. "If there has been tournament after tournament and there's really no place [for fish] to hide, you need to find something different. Sometimes I'm fortunate in that respect because 90 percent of the guys are beating the banks or beating the shallow water. So if there is a deeper bite, that'll help me. For the most part, when a lake is beat up like that, you've got to go to spinning gear using a shaky-head worm or drop-shot and just finesse out a limit.

"The main thing is not to lose your confidence and don't get negative. Stay as positive as you can no matter how many things are going wrong or how tough the fishing is. It's possible to catch up."

In the end, it all comes down to experience and instinct. "There's an instinct that I can't explain that I get. I'll go into a creek or a cove and it just looks right to me. And it usually works out that it is."

Sam Swett: "If it's a lake I've never been to and I have unlimited practice time, I'll cruise the lake. I want to determine visually what the lake has to offer. If the midsection of a lake is reported to have stained water, I want to see what they are calling 'stained water.' Sometimes it could be clear water. 'Clear water' in south Louisiana means you can see 2 or 3 feet. 'Clear water' up in New York means you can see 10 to 20 feet deep."

Swett also wants to identify the types of vegetation the water has and check out the bottom. Is it clay? Gravel? Chunk rock? He will write this type of information about a body of water on his maps. This is critical, especially if the information you find during practice isn't printed on your maps. "If the map just notes that there are ledges in a spot but I'm graphing stumps and grass on it, I'm going to write that information on the map." These kinds of detail-oriented notes on lake or river characteristics provide you with a valuable database of information that will continue to grow as you learn that body of water over time. Top-performing pros never underestimate this kind of discipline, especially early in their careers.

Swett takes notes all during practice. "Some of my maps look horrible because I make marks about anything that relates to a particular spot. If I found a brush pile, I'll want to mark that on my map and make a few notes that will give me coordinates on that spot. I don't want to rely just on my GPS. I want both my GPS and my handwritten notes to get me back to that exact spot."

Swett recalls a tournament practice he had a few years ago when he found a clearwater bayou and was throwing a spinnerbait. "I found that I could catch fish in every irregular feature in the grass line. A lot of the irregular features were caused by either a stump or a branch extending out from the shoreline that was catching the grass and making these small eddies. But you couldn't see them until you were right on top of them with the boat. I caught two or three quality fish. I just took my time and jotted down [on the map] every place I found these irregular features." That kind of detail allowed Swett to know exactly where to find each of these features and when to throw to them. It's what helped him win that tournament.

If time is limited, Swett will make an educated guess as to what section of the lake he needs to be on. "Sometimes anglers want to search one end of the lake to another and try to know everything there is about that water. Sometimes there's just not enough time." For example, pulling into a creek channel and spending your practice time getting a deeper understanding about all aspects of that creek, as opposed to blasting your way around the lake in search of water, is one strategy for managing your practice time effectively.

Slow down and carefully troll through the area, using your electronics to take note of every detail that could help you determine where the fish might be holding. If you have a very short period of time to practice, learn one section of the lake very well and find out during practice what's working in that section. In normal two- or three-day practices, Swett tries to eliminate as much water as possible so he can move into the tournament with a few select spots. The outcome from practice should be a high degree of fishing confidence in a smaller number of spots on a body of water.

During practice, Swett limits the amount of fish he will catch in a spot. His point is that he doesn't want to catch all the fish and "sore mouth" them to his baits. "Sometimes I don't even want to show the fish my bait. If they hit it and they feel that hard plastic from a jerkbait, crankbait, or something else, they might not hit it again. So if I go into a spot and catch two or three quality fish, I'll stop fishing. Then I'll start idling the boat around the area with the trolling motor to learn as much about the area as possible."

Swett believes you need to work as hard as you can during practice and feel confident about what you found. "Until you get that confidence level, keep practicing." He points out, however, that you can have a great practice and still end up not winning anything if you're in "information overload" with too much practice. Like anything else in bass tournament fishing, knowing when enough practice is enough is key to making a winning finish. "Some anglers can start second-guessing themselves as to where they should go [when the tournament starts]. That goes back to the problem of expanding too much territory during practice."

Being on a lake that is 70 miles long, where you might find fish in spots that are very distant from each other, is part of the challenge. Given the limited time you have to fish, being able to clearly decide which spots you want to focus on during the tournament is critical for winning placement. Otherwise, as Swett points out, you'll spend more time trying to decide where to fish instead of fishing.

"Really try to focus on the matter at hand. If you've had a successful practice, really define what you found." That means looking for areas that you could use for backups that are near your key fishing spots. On large bodies of water, it's a matter of determining how much fishing

You can't be intimidated by the prospect of fishing a huge lake, like Lake Erie pictured here. LURENET.COM

time you are losing by moving from spot to spot. Concentrate your efforts on just a few key areas so that you don't lose valuable fishing time. There's nothing worse than spending more time traveling than actually fishing.

Swett takes a page from pro Rick Clunn: "Rick taught me the adage 'If you think about it, do it.' Rick believes that somewhere in your past you were in a similar situation where something worked for you. Your mind recalls that somehow. You never want to be in the 'would of, could of, should of' situation. Some would plainly call that more of a 'gut feel' for approaching a certain fishing situation. Whatever you call it, it's the application of your total fishing experience that will help you win tournaments."

At the end of every practice day, Swett takes a good long walk. It helps him accomplish two important things: relieve stress and clear his head. This ultimately allows him to mentally play back the practice day with a clear focus on what happened. With a clear and stress-free mind, he's able to remember things that he might have otherwise overlooked about practice.

While pretournament research and planning is key to success, keeping an open mind is even more important, says Swett. "Always keep your mind open. Don't go into a tournament based on your pretournament information only. Make sure you let the fish, the conditions, and the environment dictate how you need to make adjustments."

Frank Scalish: Scalish believes that the best way to deal with the first practice day is to hit it hard. "You've got to get up early and be on the water when the sun is coming up. You've got to be ready to make it count. On the first practice day, you've got to spend every minute you can on the water. Sometimes, your research and hunches pay off and you immediately find the right pattern. Then you can spend the rest of your practice time honing in on your better-quality bites and/or finding more spots."

He reminds us that despite our best research and preparation, there's no substitute for fishing "in the now." "This is what the water looks like *now*. Maybe *now* is different from the last time I was here. Or maybe the water level is up or down since I did my research. Sometimes the best thing to do is not make that first cast after you launch your boat. Sometimes it's OK to sit there and drive around and look the water over."

A tournament on Smith Lake in Alabama illustrates Scalish's point: "I had never been there in my life. I started to catch a few fish in practice but nothing to write home about. What I was doing in practice was deep-jigging for spotted bass, focusing on channel bends and bluff walls. As the practice days went on, that bite was dying on me. I couldn't figure out how to be consistent. Every now and then I'd catch a good fish. On tournament day I ran to a channel bend, a bluff bend, and I start fishing and didn't get bit. I had gotten a few bites there during practice but no bites during the tournament. So I decided to work the channel out to a gravel point. I caught a 4-pounder on that gravel point. So then I decided to run secondary points, and I blasted them. I had one of the biggest stringers of the whole tournament. I had never fished any of that water in practice. It was a completely different bite, and it was the mother lode of bites.

"I got so focused on [fishing] the bluffs and channel bends that I was driving by the secondary points to get to the next channel bend or bluff. Bass break the rules, and you've got to figure them out. A failure in practice is not a failure in the tournament—it's just a way of narrowing down water."

If during practice Scalish finds a pattern that is working—for example, cranking or flipping—he'll try something else. His point is clear: Don't get stuck on just one pattern during practice that happens to be working well. Practice is time to find out what other patterns may also work.

"If I already know how to catch them, then I need to figure out how to get better-quality fish. That's tournament fishing. Tournament fishing is not a numbers game. You only need five bites, but you need the best five bites. When I won the BASS Buffalo tournament, I went out and practiced and was catching about seventy bass a day. They were all between 1.75 pounds and 2.75 pounds. After the first practice day, I went back to my room and thought: This isn't going to win it. I need

a 4-pound average [per fish] to win it. So I told myself to bail on what I was doing in practice and check something else. Sure enough, I went 20 feet deeper than I was during practice and I caught a 5-pound fish." The rest is history, as Scalish continued to find quality fish that enabled him to win the tournament.

"If I'm deep-structure fishing, usually a summer pattern or a winter pattern, and I catch one [fish], dollars-to-a-donut it's loaded with fish." Winter deepwater patterns provide access to even greater numbers of fish. "If I'm fishing shallow and flipping, I won't set up on a fish. I'll let him take the bait and pull up on it a few times to see how heavy the fish is. But I won't hook them." During practice, Scalish likes to hook only about every fifth fish or so, in order to get a good look at the quality of the fish in that spot.

"The more time you spend fishing and the more experience you have on the water, the better you can relate to conditions you'll encounter during any tournament. The minute you begin to get smarter than the fish, that's when you have problems. That's when you start second-guessing yourself instead of following what your brain and experience are telling you."

Common Practice Mistakes

There are some things that tournament anglers may do that can put a damper on their overall performance. Here are a few of the more common practice mistakes that touring bass pros witness all the time while on the water:

Over-catching fish. There's always the guy who says, "I caught fifteen fish in this spot during practice." Sure, he probably caught every one of them, but this is not a standard practice among professional bass anglers. Just catch a few and then spend the time learning the features of that particular area of water.

Going to areas that you did well in many tournaments ago. Old habits die hard, and letting go of spots that might have produced well in the past is a difficult thing to do. It's natural to have confidence in an area that has produced well for you before. Top bass pros know when to let that area go when they can't find the pattern to make it produce.

Lack of patience. Should I go or should I stay? How many times have you left an area only to hear that some anglers came after you and loaded up their boat with good fish? Or vice versa—when you stayed and the fish never turned on? "It's one of the hardest mind games that fishermen have to overcome." Most professional anglers recommend following your experience, and therefore your gut instinct, on when to stay or leave a particular spot.

To those who say, "We flipped all day and didn't catch much of anything," Scalish responds with, "Then why were you flipping all day?" He advises that if the technique you're using isn't working after an hour or so, change it to something else. "People can get caught in a

rut during practice. Practice is exactly that—practice."

Not using your electronic locator because you are fishing shallow or fishing blowdowns in shallow water. Explains Scalish, "They'll fish thirty blowdowns and catch fish on three of them. Turns out that if they had their locator on, they would have found out that there was a little ditch that ran into those three blowdowns. Had they known that, they could have idled [their boat] down that blowdown bank and put a GPS coordinate on only those blowdowns that had ditches running to them. Then when tournament time comes, they are going to fish the productive blowdowns instead of the unproductive blowdowns."

Overlooking some of the smaller, more subtle changes in structure. The only way to find those structural breaks is by using your electronics. According to Scalish, most anglers are looking for the big structural breaks, like a sharp change in depth from, say, 10 to 20 feet. "That's a good structural break, however—a structural break is any change in contour. It doesn't matter if it's 2 feet or 1 foot."

Changing lures or lure colors too often or too soon. Scalish tells the story of the angler who catches a bass on a crankbait, and it's hooked on the last treble hook: "He's got one tiny hook in his mouth; he doesn't even have the whole treble hook in his mouth. A lot of people will assume a color change will get a more aggressive bite. In some instances, that is true. The reality is, [the fish] saw that color and struck at that color. He just struck at it poorly." In this situation, Scalish will consider changing from a bait that rattles to a bait that doesn't.

Underestimating the effects of weather. "Weather can keep you from fishing," says Scalish. "Weather has kept me off of Lake Erie [for practice] because of waves and wind. It's kept me off of Santee-Cooper because of lightning storms and tornados. That can very easily happen—don't think it doesn't. The next day you can get on the water, you have to keep that storm in mind. It's going to change the water clarity in certain parts of the lake. If I want to fish the east side of the lake and the storm blew in from the west, chances are the east side of the lake is going to be muddy. That's because of the wind. The lakes down south are very susceptible to muddy water conditions. In muddy water, [the fish] don't bite very well." However, Scalish notes that lakes outside of the South that have dirty or muddy water conditions will often offer the tournament angler a great fish bite.

What to Do When Practice Doesn't Go Well

Tournament practice time can provide a different outcome for different anglers. Practice time is invaluable to the tournament pro but is also susceptible to the same variables as the tournament time itself. Changes in weather, seasonal influences, rising water or low water, and other variables can make practice seem a breeze or a nightmare. Practice is all about finding both "quality" fish (lunkers 4 pounds or better) and "limit" fish (smaller fish but many of them). With as much that can go wrong as can go right during a practice, it's the angler who can recover from a less-than-perfect practice who wins tournaments and cashes checks.

Elias: Elias doesn't confide in too many anglers when on the tour. However, there is a handful who he knows well and can discuss things with in trust and confidence. He'll take the time to compare notes with those confidants and use that information to determine his game plan for the tournament.

"When I'm not catching them [during practice], I always try to keep an open mind." He recalls a tournament where he was in the top ten after day one but fell down some after day two and was struggling on day three. "I just decided that if I'm going down, I'm going down swinging, doing what I'm best at and enjoy doing. So I went out and started throwing a crankbait, and I caught a 20-pound stringer and won the tournament. Normally, when I'm struggling during a tournament, I'll rely on my [fishing] strengths and bear down with that.

"If I've spent two and a half days practicing and I've done no good, I'm not going to go out there, do the same thing, and expect a different result. I'm going to change up, make a decision, put my trolling motor down, and go fishing. I'm not going to run and gun. A high percentage of the time it'll work out if you put your trolling motor down and fish."

Mason: "If a practice doesn't go well, then you have to make a decision: Do I pick another section of the lake? Or do I try to find the fish in the section I originally picked? I'm about fifty-fifty on that." Mason will remain in an area if he feels that its history shows that it is a strong fish producer. What he changes is his approach to fishing that area.

"There are different ways to approach [a bad practice]. You have one of two options: You either start the next day as a practice day, or go to the areas on the lake that fit your most confident style of fishing. Most of the time, I'll look for areas where I can fish a shallow crankbait and cover a lot of water quickly. What that does is allow you to fish isolated, shallow targets in a manner that you're covering a lot of water." Mason doesn't hesitate to put a shaky-head worm on and finesse fish if practice hasn't gone well. "Generally, when you do those techniques all day, you'll catch enough [fish] to survive."

Mason believes that one of the most important things you can do in a bad practice situation is to stay calm. "Settle down and fish. You're not going to catch any fish running around all day. If you are struggling and you don't have anything going, the worst thing you could do is run and fish one spot for five minutes and then fish another one for five minutes.

"A good example of that is the first major tournament I ever won. It was the American Bass Anglers National Championship back in 2003. I did not have the greatest practice, and the bad thing was it was on my home lake. It was on Wheeler Lake with about 500 people in the tournament. It was a really big event. First place was $60,000, so at the time, it was the biggest tournament I had ever fished. After the practice, my only goal was to get a check. I wanted to finish in the top 50. That night at the registration meeting, I drew boat number one. Driving home, I knew that I had first shot at any spot I wanted on that lake, so I basically picked the areas I had the most confidence in and went to first. Within two or three casts, I caught a nice fish and started the morning off well. I caught three nice fish in the morning. So within the first hour, I went from having a fairly tough practice to having three nice fish in the live well. That kind of cued me in to what other places I knew were just like that. By the end of the day, I put together a nice bag [of fish]."

Mason was the leader for all three days and won the tournament by 9 pounds. "That was the win that started my career."

Howell: "You have to fish every day as if it's your first day, with no preconceived notions. On the third day of practice, I'll go out and figure out what I'm going to do." A lot of times, a pro like Howell finds himself figuring out the pattern for getting bites in the last few hours of practice.

■ Jimmy Mason applies what he learned during pretournament practice to gain a significant competitive edge. LURENET.COM

In a sense then, there is no such thing as bad practice day. You've just spent two or three days eliminating water that is not productive for you, and your best strategy is to fish the water that you haven't already eliminated. Howell points out that repeating what already didn't work in practice is a plan for tournament disaster.

On Lake Wheeler in 1998 during an FLW event, he clearly remembers a less-than-satisfactory practice that turned itself around. It was also the tour event that earned him $100,000 and propelled his bass-fishing career. During this tour, Howell had five whole days of practice available to him. "I caught five bass in five days, and three of those bass were caught on one day! So I had three days where I didn't catch a fish." This was a critical event, primarily because he was on the short end of the financial strap. "We were really in debt and needing to make this event."

Howell continues, "I went out to this area that I wanted to fish and the wind was blowing big whitecaps across this flat. I couldn't fish it because it was so windy. But every time I went by there [during practice], I had a gut feeling that I needed to be fishing out there." He never was able to pick up a fish in that flat during practice, but the next morning of the tournament, he had that gut feeling again that he should fish it. "So I went onto this flat, the wind wasn't blowing, and starting throwing a Rat-L-Trap. . . . Right off the bat, I caught a good fish, then a 5-pounder. Then I caught a few more."

Howell was focusing his attention on little patches of grass that he found in the flat, and he put together a good pattern for that location. The result was about 15-plus pounds of fish on the first day, and he was leading the event! "The second day I go out and start fishing around [the flat] and didn't get a bite. I started moving around and found another little patch of grass out in some stumps." In short order, another limit was on board his boat. With those two catches, he was able to make the top-ten cut.

By the time Howell got to the third day, the wind had kicked up again, making it impossible to fish that flat-water area. "I moved around [the lake] again and found another little patch of fish and caught another 9.5-pound limit." This allowed him to make the cut and fish against the likes of Rick Clunn, Tommy Biffle, and Larry Nixon. "It was all the big dogs and little old me that nobody knew."

On the last day of the tournament, conditions changed again and Howell could not catch fish where he had caught them the day before. He managed to catch four, and in the last minute and a half before he had to check in, he decided to make one last cast. That cast caught his fifth and last fish, and it weighed in at 2.5 pounds. "I checked in with twenty seconds to spare and no camera boat in sight to record that last fish. The only guy who saw me catch it was the check-in boat. I ended up beating Rick Clunn by one ounce." It just goes to show that it doesn't matter what or how you do in practice, it's what you do in the tournament that counts.

Swett: If he's not doing well during practice, Swett will sometimes employ the "bent rod" pattern. That's when he tries to learn what pattern is causing nearby anglers to get into fish, hence the "bent rod." "If I'm doing well during a practice, I'm not particularly concerned about other fishermen. But you always want to be aware of your environment. When you're on a tournament lake, other fishermen are part of that environment. You need to be aware of that. You don't bank on that, but you need to be aware of what's going on around you.

"Most of the guys out here on tour, they know the [seasonal] patterns. They know what's going on [in a body of water]. Generally, the person who wins the tournament has found something that is a little different that takes fish. We all have our seasonal patterns and our favorite baits to throw, but so do a hundred to two hundred other guys doing the very same thing and looking at the same water. They all have relatively the same information. Sometimes during practice, the very best school of fish can sort of get beat up a bit. They can get a lot of pressure and get hooked in the process." In this case, a slight adjustment may mean the difference between winning and losing. That adjustment could be as simple as varying the color, size, or speed of retrieve of your bait. It could mean changing the angle at which you cast and retrieve your bait in relation to where the fish are staging, or it could be a slight change in fish movement from one kind of structure to another.

Scalish: "A bad practice is not necessarily bad. A bad practice is telling you that whatever you're doing isn't working. So the next day you need to do exactly the opposite." Scalish suggests starting your "practice time" over during the tournament. "You start right where you left off and do things differently during the tournament. Some of the best tournaments you can have, you can also have the worst practice days in."

CHAPTER FOUR

Developing Your Tournament Strategy

Developing the right tournament strategy is the key to increasing your chances for a win, or at least a check. Tournament strategy is a multifaceted plan that has several parts: 1) where you want to fish, 2) when you want to fish, 3) how you want to fish, and 4) what baits you want to fish with.

Ask successful tournament professionals what role strategy plays in their success, and they'll tell you it is a critical part of it. After days of practice, having a solid strategy for winning the tournament is the foundation for getting there. However, strategy has an Achilles heel: change.

What if the weather dramatically changes? What if the pattern you've developed in practice draws yawns from the bass during the first day of the tournament? What if your boat breaks down right in the middle of the tournament? The list of "what if" variables can go on and on.

You can have the most logical performance- and experience-based strategy, but any kind of variable can put a big kink in it. Then you have to do something that is rarely talked about in popular fishing magazines: You have to make decisions.

Sometimes a few, sometimes many, but you will have to make them.

Besides developing the ability to come up with a solid strategy for winning a tournament, you need to focus on becoming a highly effective decision-maker. There is no one right way to develop, execute, or readjust your tournament strategy. It's a personal journey that is shaped and sharpened by only one thing: experience.

Tournament Strategy Options

Jimmy Mason: Mason is big on being mentally organized as he puts his tournament strategy together. "Stuff becomes more real when I write it down. I organize myself so much better when I write it down. Each day during practice I'm making notes, and each night I'll organize my notes. The night before a tournament, I'll go through my notes and write out a fresh list of goals, which are the areas I want to fish during the day, in the order I plan to fish them. Basically, I like to make an outline of what I expect to be doing the next day. As I do this, I'm picturing the day unfolding [during the tournament]. At the

▥ **Jimmy Mason will make detailed notes regarding key areas he wants to prioritize and fish during his practice time.** DAVID DIRKS

same time, I'm keeping an open mind and am ready for anything."

Writing out his strategy gives Mason a sense of confidence and lowers his anxiety level before the tournament. It seems to make sense. If you have a plan or outline of what you want to do, then you'll have at least a stronger start. Compare that to someone who does no planning before the tournament and just "wings it." You might expect that person's anxiety level to be just a bit higher.

Terry Scroggins: "If you go to one particular spot on your home body of water, you can't catch [fish] four days in a row off of it. So don't come out to a brand-new lake and try to do it. It won't work. Don't be afraid to fish new water. That's the number one key. If you look at all the big-name guys out here [on the tour] that do really well, you'll see that they don't stay in one spot. They cover a lot of water, and they are not afraid to move forward and see what's ahead of them. You can't get hung up on what happened yesterday. Keep moving and swing for the fence on the move.

"Ninety percent of the guys out here can look at a lake and say, 'That's where the fish should be.' And that's right. But when we come to an event that's a week long, with three days of practice and four days of tournament, those places get hammered. So what you've got to do is find some off-the-wall, key places that nobody is going to find. Those spots are not going to be as good as, say, a point, a super-ledge, or a

bridge piling, but over a four-day period, those places are going to get beat up. Then they become no good as spots. Catching one or two fish on a particular spot might not be considered very good, but those one or two fish will make a difference. These tournaments are won by ounces. Very seldom does someone get blown away by 3 or 4 pounds. Those two or three fish could make a very big difference."

Scroggins believes that if your strategy is not playing out during the tournament, the best thing to do is not worry about the last cast, just think about the one you're getting ready to make. "That happened to me this year. I lost two fish in the last thirty minutes of a tournament. I finished second but would have won it if I had caught either one of those fish. You can't get caught up in that. Stay focused on moving ahead."

Tournament fishing is not just about trying to win for money, it's also about accumulating points that you'll need to stay in the game. "When you come out here and fish the Elite Series, Open Series, or FLW Series, it's all points-related. Before a tournament starts, everybody has the mind-set to win it. They are trying to win the event, but sometimes that doesn't work. You can't always swing for a home run. If things are not working, you need a backup plan where you can go and catch a small limit [of fish] to keep those points up. That's important. When I go out to practice, I try to find big fish. I know and everybody knows that isn't going to happen every time. Along with finding those big fish, I try to find numbers of fish as well."

Scroggins stresses that the tournament-fishing business is like any other business and that it takes three to five years to get established. "You start learning these bodies of water. When you do find a spot, you mark it on your electronics and it's there for life." Over time you'll accumulate a number of spots on your electronics gear that will make your fishing more efficient and effective. But again, there's no replacing real time and experience on the water.

"I've been fishing BASS since 2001, and the older guys are saying, 'Man, the competition is getting so much greater now.' The reason why is the electronics [we have] today. That's what is making anglers so much better." Scroggins points out that it's much more challenging, if not impossible, for a newcomer to the tours to make it quickly. This is primarily due to the fact that many of the pros on the tour have five, ten, twenty, or more years in tournament fishing. "They've seen that lake fifty times more than you have. You're not going to go in there and beat them overnight."

Paul Elias: Elias recommends keeping your strategy as basic as possible. "Look at the time of the year. It's pretty much known what the fish are doing in each part of the year. My way of doing it is I would pick one area of the lake and concentrate on that area. I wouldn't spend a bunch of time trying to cover the whole lake. If you

go with a preconceived notation about how you're going to fish or what lure you're going to catch them on, you're trying to force-feed the fish something that's not really working. So I will go to the lake with about fifteen rods rigged up and try to get the fish to show me what they are doing."

Elias considers rising water his toughest tournament-fishing challenge. "Get to the bank," he advises. "I don't care if you have to go through twenty acres of flooded timber to get there, you better find some way to get to the bank." Failing that, he says, you probably won't do very well. He also tries to locate riprap and works to establish a pattern that will produce a bite, especially during cold, rising water situations. When a lake is 5 feet above normal, the two main places Elias concentrates on are the old shoreline and the new [existing] shoreline.

Frank Scalish: "Always go to your best fish first. I hear guys saying, 'They won't bite until the afternoon.' Maybe you didn't find them in practice until the afternoon. And what if someone beats you to those fish and they wind up catching the mother lode at 6:30 in the morning? You have to go to your best fish first, period." Scalish points out that if you don't get a bite on those best spots in the morning, you can always return to them in the afternoon. "It's about pattern fishing, not about spots, so you have to be open-minded in the tournament. You're going to go to your best fish first and play it by ear. If you run to spot A and somebody is on it, you go to spot B.

"What you have to keep an eye on is pattern changes during a tournament. You may get to your A spot where you caught them [in practice] on deepwater cranking. You go there and you only catch one [on cranking]. Maybe the fish are now suspended in the water column and they're not relating to the bottom anymore. So you have to put on a midrange crankbait or drop-shot them."

Scalish classifies fishing spots into three categories: A, B, and C. "An A spot does not mean a limit [of fish]. It's a spot where I can catch giant fish or at least bigger [fish] than what I've been catching. To me, size matters. A B spot has a decent grade of fish and maybe I'll catch a few numbers [of fish] there. A C+ spot is where I can get a few bites. They're keepers but it's nothing to write home about. . . . A limit spot is a spot where I know I can go in there and catch five. Usually, with the limit spots, they are not the first places I run to if I'm sure I can catch five fish anytime I go there." For a useful way to chart your spots, see appendix B.

Scalish says that the type of structure and cover you're fishing should dictate your bait choices. "The water color is going to dictate your color choices. Good rule of thumb: When you're throwing soft plastics, match the soft plastics to the color of the water. If the water looks kind of green, throw a green pumpkin or watermelon. If the water looks brown, throw a green

pumpkin or something dark. The clearer the water, the more translucent the plastic. The dirtier the water, the more solid [in color] the soft plastic should be."

Making Decisions—The Real Key to Success

Ask any bass pro what role decision-making plays in tournament success, and their reply will sound a lot like Randy Howell's: "That's the hardest part of tournament fishing. That's the part that separates the winners from the losers and the guys who make a lot of money from the guys who make a little money [on the tour]."

For even more clarity on the subject of tournament decision-making, listen to what Elias says: "I really believe that the decision side of the game can make you feel like a king or jump up and bite you in the butt."

Effective decision-making (that is, doing the right things to put fish in the boat) is not a topic you'll find in many bass books or magazine articles. There's a mountain of fishing advice available that doesn't add up to much if you can't figure out the "when" part of the equation: When do you decide to "run and gun" for another spot? Do you "stay and play" in a spot that hasn't produced much in the past three hours of tournament time? When is it time to switch tactics?

You can read all you want about how to use certain baits, fish the seasonal patterns, and find structure, along with the proverbial "10 Ways to Fish Cover." At the end of the day, however, it's your ability to make the right decisions that will propel you to a win or, at the very least, a check.

Scalish: Decision-making during a tournament is a combination of art and science, with more art than science to it. "The more time you spend [fishing], the better your decision-making becomes. You can't be a tournament pro overnight." Scalish likens the process of becoming a successful tournament angler to learning how to become a great public speaker. "If you want to get really good at public speaking, you've got to figure out how many times the average guy speaks [publicly] in a year. Then go do that ten times more in a year. Then you've got ten years' experience in one year."

Scalish points out the difference between local tournament fishing and the professional level of bass fishing. Anglers who fish the same local lakes "fish five tournaments a year and they're all on the same lakes. They start to do well on those lakes after a while because those are the lakes they fish. So they sit there and say, 'I can do it. I can be a tournament pro.' But what they don't realize is that touring tournament pros are seeing twelve different lakes, twelve different times a year, and different lakes every year with two days of practice. There's a big difference. You have to have the ability in practice to really cover water and really understand what you're catching or [why] not."

Scalish offers the following advice on deciding whether to run and gun or stay and play: "The pattern is going to dictate how I'm going to fish. If I'm fishing crankbaits on secondary points, I'm running and gunning like crazy. If I'm fishing deepwater brush piles, I'm running and gunning because I have to cover as much [water] as I can. If I'm structure fishing channel ledges or deep breaks, I'm going to take more time on those spots because it's all about the angle of your cast and hitting the sweet spot. That's the whole key to structure fishing—the angle of your cast. A lot of guys pull up on a hump or a rock pile and they'll make a few casts and say, 'There's nothing here,' and they'll leave. You could pull up on that same place and turn the boat around and load the boat because the angle of the cast is different and it's the right angle. So you're going to take a little bit more time with that stuff."

Successful structure fishing requires that you pay attention and let the fish tell you how they want the bait. It can sometimes simply take a subtle change in the angle of the bait presentation to make a fish bite. In a tournament, this could mean the difference between coming home and coming home with a check. "If you're sitting around begging fish to bite, you are probably not going to catch them. If you're on the right pattern, doing the right thing, you are going to get bit. If you're not getting bit, it's time to go."

There are a couple other variables that Scalish likes to narrow down: "Am I doing

■ Jerkbaits, like these XCalibur Twitch baits, mimic mortally wounded baitfish. When the crankbaits aren't working, try a jerkbait instead. DAVID DIRKS

poorly by not making the top-ten cut? Am I doing poorly by not getting a check? Or do I need a big day to qualify for the Classic? Let's say I'm doing poorly and if I catch a couple of fish, I'm guaranteed ten grand. But if I blank, I won't get the ten grand. Then I'm going to fish conservatively to get the ten grand. Let's say I have a chance to make the top-twelve cut for television and if I don't catch them very well, I'm not going to fall out of the $10K spot. Then I'm going to press—I'm going to do what I know how to do to catch a bigger bite and hopefully creep up to the number ten

slot. If I have a chance to make the Classic, and I need to really make a comeback, I'm going to fish for big fish. If I flip a lizard, I catch a lot of 1- or 2-pound fish, but if I put a big jig on with a Super Spook, I know I'm only going to get four bites a day but they'll be 7-pound fish, then I'll take that chance."

At Florida's Lake Tohopekaliga (aka Lake Toho) in 2007, that's exactly what Scalish did. "I was guaranteed $10K, but I was catching 1- to 1.5-pound fish. I had a spot where I could get a limit of 1-pounders, and I was in seventeenth place. One-pounders were not going to put me in the top ten, and I'm not going to fall out of getting a check—I already made the check cut. So I went flipping for nothing but big fish. I ended up catching two little ones, and that was that. I went for the big bites knowing that I wasn't going to get a limit but if I caught one, it would equal most guys' 1-pound limit if I got one big bite. So I decided to go for broke. I had nothing to lose money-wise but everything to gain if I could make the television cut."

Mason: "When you fish a lake a lot,

you begin to form opinions about different areas. Lake Guntersville is one of my home lakes and when I'm not fishing tournaments, it's one of the lakes I spend a lot of time on. The area on Guntersville that Kevin VanDam won a tournament in during 2007 was such a huge community hole, I never fished it in practice. Very few local tournaments are ever won off of it because it's fished so heavily. It's just not one of the better areas to fish. On the map the area looks perfect, but it gets so much local pressure that I really underestimated

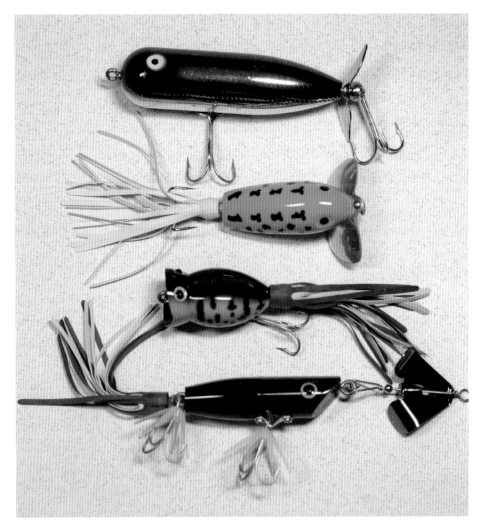

◼ There are many times when a morning or evening topwater bite will bring fish into the boat. Deciding when to use specific baits comes with time and experience.
DAVID DIRKS

it. Because of my knowledge of the lake, I underestimated what would really be there, but that's where VanDam won the tournament." Lesson: Never overlook or underestimate the obvious.

Using a Lake Toho tournament in 2007 as an example, Mason illustrates the entire cycle from practice to tournament play: "Lake Toho was a very tough situation. September in Florida is always tough. Everybody knew it was going to be the lowest-catch tournament of the year. First day of practice, I had three bites; I caught two keepers. The second day I decided to spend my time on the lake two lakes down [from Toho]. I caught some small fish but never really found what I wanted until midday.

"Midday I went into a creek that fed into the lake. It had a really fast-flowing current. The water was about 10 degrees cooler, and it was falling really fast. In the first hour I had about fifteen bites. I knew I had found a great area, as tough as it was down there. Then I go and try to replicate that, as there were three other creeks on that lake. I went to all of them and I had a few bites, so I knew I had one good area and one fallback or secondary area to fish." He and his partner decided to go to the next lake down from Toho, Tiger Lake.

Fishing Tiger Lake, they found it had a great topwater bite. Tiger produced about ten bites in the last three hours of the day. Mason and his partner were both fishing topwater baits near the shoreline grass, and Mason noted that the fish they caught

during this time were quality fish: "I felt I had an area that I could pound hard and get some quality fish." The second day of practice went pretty much the same as the first day. "I was feeling a lot better after the second day. On the third day [of practice], I was back on Lake Toho again and tried to fish some areas I had fished in the past." He struggled during this last and final practice before the tournament began.

"That night, when I reviewed my practice, I found that the creek I had fished the first day [of practice] that had flowing water had the most concentrated number of bites. I knew it was going to be one of those tournaments where every fish counted. I also knew it was probably going to take about 8 pounds [of fish] a day to finish in fiftieth [place] and get $10,000." Mason's plan was to hit the creek first, knowing he could get a limit first thing in the morning on day one of the tournament. Next, his strategy was to go to Tiger Lake and work the topwater frog that had brought him several quality fish during practice. He was counting on the quality fish from Tiger to help him cull some of the smaller fish from his Lake Toho limit.

When the tournament began, Mason went into action, executing his plan. When he arrived at the creek, he found another angler already there—game over on that spot. "I spun around and headed straight to Tiger Lake. For whatever reason, the fishing there wasn't nearly as good as we encountered [during practice]. So I go in there and fish until about 10:30

a.m. I caught one, a 3-pounder. It was a good-quality fish for down there." Mason then wheeled around and went back to the creek he visited in the morning. He found out later that morning that the angler who was there before him had caught 10 pounds of fish.

His next move was to head back up to Lake Toho and start fishing the grass mats with a frog. In the next few hours, he caught seven keeper fish. After making some culls, he had a five-fish limit for the day with about 9 pounds of fish for the first day of the tournament. A top-fifty place was about 6 pounds of fish, so he knew he was ahead of his plan for cashing a check. The running and gunning he did on the first day, round-trip, was about 90 miles.

The second day of the tournament was about to begin and Mason needed to come up with a plan to keep his momentum going. The grass mat he had been fishing was only about 2 miles from the boat ramp. "I made a decision that I had never done at that level before. I went to the grass mat and never cranked it up until it was time to come in. I basically fished a 100-yard stretch back and forth for eight and a half hours. I ended up catching another 9 pounds, which put me in twenty-fourth place [on day two]."

Making the top-fifty cut allowed Mason to fish the third day of the tournament. "The next day, I gambled. I knew that there was not enough fish in the mat, or enough quality fish to make the top twelve

and get to fish the fourth day." So, on the third day, Mason ran back down to Tiger Lake and changed his technique. Instead of fishing topwater, he went to flipping a YUM Dinger, basically against the sparse vegetation. "Then I caught a 4-pounder, which is a good-quality fish. I did that for another three and a half hours and never had another bite. A little after noon, I ran back up to the mats and worked a frog fish and caught my limit." Needless to say, Mason ended up completing the Toho tournament in twenty-fifth place and took home a check.

There are a number of lessons here. Rather than continuing to run and gun to multiple spots, Mason ended up focusing on the fish-producing ability of one or two key areas. Long stretches between bites didn't deter him from fishing those areas for hours at a time until they produced the results he needed to win a check. He remained calm despite some practice-time setbacks and methodically fished the spots that he had a high degree of confidence in until they produced fish.

Howell: Howell looks at decision-making during a tournament this way: Either you make the right decisions, or you have to make your decisions right. "If you make a decision to run 50 miles upriver to flip trees, that's your decision, your commitment. If after three hours you've only caught one fish, your head starts playing mind games on you. Then you starting thinking, well, am I going to catch them or not? Do I need to keep doing this? Or do I throw this [pattern] out and do something else?"

If the decision is made to run 50 miles upriver and it's not working, Howell's strategy is to figure out how to make that decision work. "Even though it might not have been the right decision, I've got to make that decision right. I've got to figure out how to make that decision work for me. That's when you have to have confidence in your ability."

He emphasizes relying on your experience to tell you what has worked or not worked in this type of situation before. Once again, when it comes to fishing successfully, there is no substitute for time on the water and the experience it brings.

The amount of time available can also be an important factor in the decision-making process. In local tournaments, anglers only have about eight hours to make one or two key decisions about where to fish and how to fish it. That tight fishing time doesn't give you a lot of room to correct decisions that didn't work out.

"I've caught myself many times in a tough fishing day when my pattern is not working and my areas are not good. And then you think, well, I heard that so-and-so caught fish everywhere he went in 10-foot-deep water on a Carolina rig on points. Then I'll try that for an hour or two and not catch anything. Then your confidence is totally gone. You've lost everything you worked on during practice and now you're chasing somebody else's information that

usually is not accurate. I've learned to stay out of all that."

Elias: "I've had a lot of times when I've left an area, deciding the fish aren't going to do it, and I've got to go somewhere else. I've had friends of mine tell me I wasn't gone more than fifteen minutes and [the fish] turned on and everybody caught a limit. I ended up running and gunning and didn't have a very good day. I believe it's really an instinct thing. The guys that make those choices well are the guys that come out on top. You really have to determine how much weight it is going to take to win this tournament and the quality of fish in the area you are fishing. It's not hard to run off and leave an area where five fish are going to weigh 10 pounds. But it is hard to run off and leave an area knowing that if you catch five, they are going to weigh 20 pounds. So, you pull up and catch one 4- or 5-pounder right off the bat and then you go two hours without a bite. You start thinking: Do I need to get out of here and go finish a limit with that 5-pound kicker? Or do I stay and hope they turn on? Most of the time, I just stay."

But what if it's the last day of the tournament and you're behind? In this case, Elias takes a different track. From his point of view, if it takes 10 pounds a day to make a check and you're catching 5 pounds a day, in a two-day tournament, you're already 10 pounds behind. That tells you that you need a 20-pound day to get a check. Do you then stay focused on what you know you can do—that is, produce a 10-pound-

Developing Your Tournament Strategy

plus stringer and maintain the points you can—or do you go for broke and try for the bigger fish, possibly zeroing out with a lot fewer points?

"I'm the kind of person that's going to change up and do something different and try to catch some big fish. If I zero, I zero. If I get one bite, I might get as much weight as I've been catching in the last two days. I'm going to go for the bigger sack."

Sam Swett's advice is to avoid going from "hero to zero." "If you look at [tournament] history, very seldom does a guy leading the tournament on the first day win the tournament. You have to make a decision on how to manage your fish. Hopefully your first five fish are good fish. If not, do you stay and cull up and take the chance of not catching anything tomorrow because you've caught basically the whole school of fish? Or you sore-lipped them all or spooked the school. That's when you see a guy go from 'hero to zero.' They'll come in with a 22- or 23-pound sack of fish. You'll hear them bragging, 'I caught twenty or thirty fish today.' Then they come in the next day and blank out, mainly because they caught them all the first day. They didn't conserve their fish."

A lot of it depends on the type of tournament you're fishing, says Swett. "If you're fishing a cumulative-weight tournament, where you take the weight you had into the 'top ten' day, or, like the FLW, where if you make it into the top ten, your previous weights are erased. Then everybody starts from ground zero." This requires you to calculate into your tournament strategy what you'll need to do in order to deal with both cumulative-weight and zeroed-weight tournaments.

Fishing with a Co-angler

Many tournaments, especially BASS and FLW tours, require a co-angler with you in the boat. There are two sides to this coin. One side is a great time for both the tournament angler and the co-angler, who coexist and make it work to their advantage. The other side of the coin is a negative experience, primarily for the co-angler. Reports of tournament anglers treating their co-anglers badly are not rumors—it happens. If you have to fish with a co-angler in your boat, the best strategy is to figure out how to make it work to your advantage.

Your co-angler can be a gauge for such things as color, size, and/or weight variances on baits. If they are outfishing you, ask yourself: What are they doing differently? Are they using a different size line weight? A 4-inch versus 6-inch bait? Try to modify your presentation to imitate what your co-angler is doing for success.

Elias: "My advice is to be as courteous as you can be to the guy in the back of the boat. At the same time, do all you can do to get your five fish in the boat first. That's what I've done before: get a good limit first and then ease up and let the guy catch some fish.

"I've had several times where my partner was throwing something different than what I was throwing and started catching fish. . . . I won a Super Bass tournament on Lake Okeechobee where I was flipping and got behind the first day. The second day I felt I needed to flip again just because of the potential of catching a big bag [of fish] and catching up. I saw a fish chasing a shad out in open water. I wasn't going to go out there and fish, but I changed my mind and made a short pass there. I was throwing a lipless crankbait." Elias was just about ready to leave that area when his partner caught a 2-pound fish. That was enough for Elias to revaluate his decision to leave the area for another spot. "I started throwing it out there, letting it go to the bottom and working it like a worm, and caught the heck out of fish and won the tournament."

Howell: "I found out over the years that it's best to treat people the way you want to be treated. A lot of pros won't even tell their partners what kind of tackle they have rigged. I hear so many bad stories from guys [amateurs] that fish with me. I tell my partner what I'm doing, how I'm fishing, and what kind of tackle I have rigged up, including baits, colors. He's going to be in the boat with me for eight hours, so I'm not going to lie to him."

Don't become a jerk. As someone once said, "Be nice to the people on your way up because they are the same people you meet on your way down." No truer words have ever been spoken. The worst thing a pro can do to an amateur is to blindside him and keep him in the dark. A pro with a reputation for treating amateur boat partners badly soon learns that his reputation will leak and become known to everyone over time.

Howell makes it a point to let his co-angler know that he'll not only keep him informed on changes he makes, but also share baits with him as well. "Most of the [co-anglers] know that we're fishing for a living, so they are not going to push you too hard. They are going to fish and do their own things."

Howell wants his co-anglers to be successful. "If they catch fish behind, I take that as a positive thing." It's another competitive edge that can factor into a win and getting a tournament check. "As soon as someone catches one fish behind me, I try to figure out right away, 'Why did he catch that fish behind me?' That is especially true when the co-angler catches two fish in a row, fishing in the same area that you've just covered minutes ago. What kind of bait does your co-angler have on, and how is he fishing it?"

Using Your Electronics

While modern fish-finding electronics won't win you a tournament, they will help you to find and identify the structure that bass are relating to. To a tournament professional, the workhorse of their "tool set" is their electronics. The combination of sonar, GPS capability, and mapping software like Navionics is the best fusion of technology and tournament fishing. As

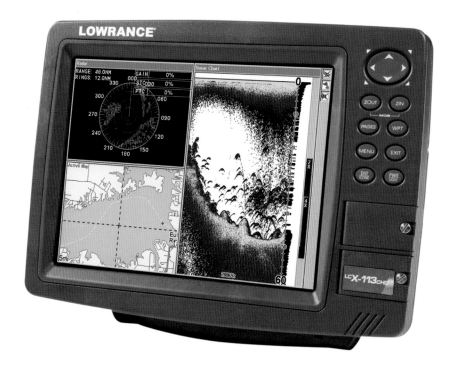

■ **Good electronics with sonar and GPS combined is a must-have for any successful tournament angler today.** NAVICO, INC.

they idle along a lake or river, tournament anglers have one eye glued to their screens and the other driving the boat.

It's a given then that if you want to compete successfully in tournaments, you need to have at least a basic electronics package on your boat. Some bass pros use a combination of hard-copy maps and their electronics, while others rely entirely on their electronics to mark key structure and fishing spots. The following tips will help you leverage your electronics for tournament success:

■ Make sure you know everything about your electronics package. You should know as much about how your sonar and GPS work as the manufacturer does, maybe even more.

■ Always check your electronics before

you leave the dock. All that technology is useless if you can't put it to work during practice or tournament time.

■ Take advantage of all the data that today's modern fishing electronics packages provide you. Many models track basic weather patterns, including barometric pressure, which is a key variable in any tournament during any season.

■ Fishing electronics units that provide wide area coverage let you cover more area in less time. This is critical, especially during practice time, when you want to discover as many fish-holding spots as possible each day.

■ Use your electronics to eliminate unproductive areas. Featureless areas of the lake bottom aren't generally productive, and your electronics can help you eliminate them from your list of potential areas to fish during the tournament.

▥ Units with 2D and 3D capability allow you to hold your boat position over underwater structure. Being able to see where your boat is in relation to the structure helps you determine how you will fish it: Do you need to back your boat off? Which side is optimal for your first approach?

▥ Use your electronics to follow along structure like contours, submerged creek beds, and drop-offs.

▥ Your electronics can help you locate schools of baitfish. Wherever there are baitfish, the bass can't be far behind.

▥ Higher-resolution screens help reduce the chances of false readings. Models with more pixels will help you distinguish between what is real and what's not. Don't skimp on power either. Most bass pros agree that a quality unit should have at least 3,000 watts of power. More power adds up to a faster reading of data (what it sees on the bottom of the lake or river) and greater accuracy.

▥ Marking every key fishing location is one thing, but using a marker or color that helps you identify or differentiate them later is critical for tournament fishing.

CHAPTER FIVE

Favorite Tournament Tactics of the Pros

"Play to your strengths" is probably the soundest advice a tournament pro can heed in the midst of the competitive battle for the heaviest weight of fish. Survey any of the top twenty-five BASS or FLW touring pros, and you'll find a majority of the consistent winners stay on top because they play to their strengths whenever they can. They understand every aspect and nuance related to their tournament and check-winning tactics, and they continue to learn and gain more experience each year they

■ **Terry Scroggins punches through thick vegetation searching for bass that other anglers will pass by.** LURENET.COM

fish. Yes, they also know how to exploit other fishing tactics, but they never forget what has brought them their success.

The season will certainly be a big influence and will determine what tactics you'll use in any tournament. That said, year after year our six pros use certain tactics in multiple seasons. Seasonal influence will only tell you where the fish are. Deciding which baits to use is generally based on how well you know how to use them to catch bass.

Terry Scroggins

"I'm from Florida, and that's where I learned how to fish. In Florida everything is shallow water [fishing]. Naturally, I'm better at fishing shallow water than water that is 30 or 40 feet deep. My number one technique is flipping grass cover, and that works all over the country. It's easy for me to come to a lake and ride around the lake and see grass floating on top of the water. It's visible. You don't have to search for it. As far as your electronics, you can go 50 miles an hour and cover a lake and see if there is any [grass] available. The downfall of that is that everybody else can see it.

"Take Lake Guntersville, for example. It's just full of grass. When I go there, that's what I look for. And I treat the grass mats just like I'm going down a creek. You want to fish all the points, the pockets, and the isolated mats. What I do is get the biggest weight available that I can get through the cover [grass]. I want to get my

bait in where someone else can't. Look for the things that everyone else is going to overlook, or they don't have the drive [it takes] to get in there.

"Let's say you have a big grass mat and everybody is fishing outside of it. On the inside of it, let's say the middle, there might be a little hole or a thicker matting of grass. You have to take the initiative and go in there and get to it. A lot of guys won't do that. They'll overlook it. You have to find things that everybody overlooks."

For punching through and working thick grass mats, Scroggins likes to use the YUM Big Show Craw, which was specifically designed for this purpose. Punching through grass allows him to find those bass that will react to his bait that's crashing through the thick mat. It's the reaction bite that gets him the fish he needs to win tournaments. In grass, Scroggins notes, "Tubes work really well."

When flipping heavy cover, you need dark colors: black/blue, black/neon, and brown/orange. "With thick grass, it's dark down there. It doesn't matter what the water clarity is, it's dark in that stuff." Scroggins goes on to say that "the number one mistake people make when flipping heavy cover when they get a fish is pull him out of there. You need to go in there and get him." He means reaching into the thick grass mat and grabbing the fish out. "Set the hook, get him hung up [in the grass], and go dig him out."

To find the right weight that will work in the grass mats he's fishing, Scroggins will

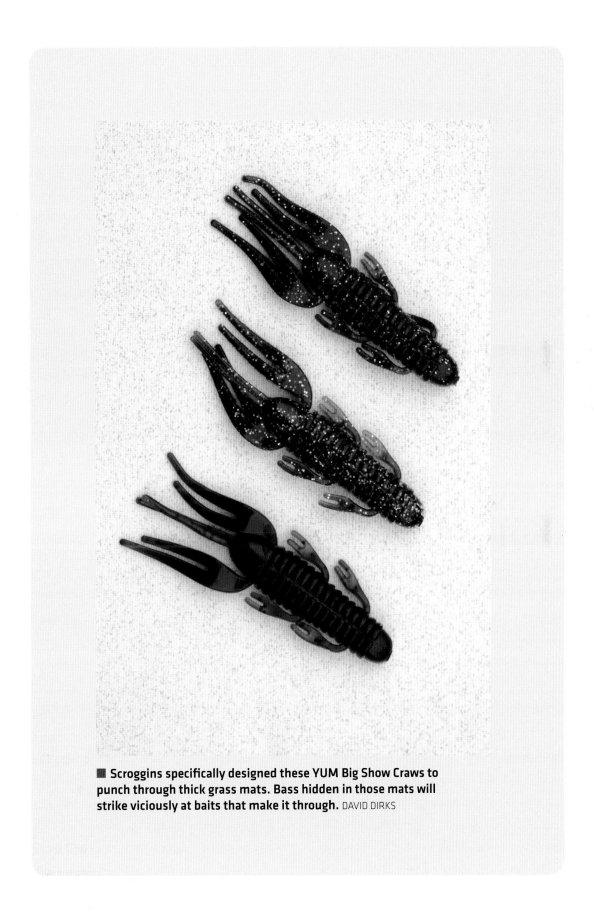

Scroggins specifically designed these YUM Big Show Craws to punch through thick grass mats. Bass hidden in those mats will strike viciously at baits that make it through. DAVID DIRKS

▌ Scroggins recommends pulling fish out of thick vegetation by hand instead of using your rod and risk losing a quality fish. LURENET.COM

rig four flipping rods with four different weights—1½ ounces, ¾ ounce, ½ ounce, and ¼ ounce—and all tungsten sinkers. He then sets the reels up with 65-pound braided line and uses 5/0 hooks. "The reason I use four different weights is the rate of fall going in through the cover. You want a weight that will go through the cover freely and doesn't slow the bait down—you want it natural going through there."

If the grass is sparse and/or more broken up, he'll switch from braid to fluorocarbon lines. A good rule of thumb on what types of line to use on grass mats:

"Anything up to a ¾-ounce weight, I use fluorocarbon. Anything over, I use braid." He uses a 7½-foot flipping rod that's has a medium/heavy to heavy action.

Sight fishing during the spawn is another key technique that Scroggins will employ across multiple tournaments. If the tournament schedule allows it, you can find yourself fishing through the spring spawning period from February (for example, in Florida) all the way through June (in New York). During the spawn, Scroggins will sometimes use his "tomato stakes" technique on the last day of practice and in the

Scroggins lifts another hefty bass from the thick lily pads using a Texas-rigged YUM Craw Pappy. LURENET.COM

last few hours. Using a cut piece of wood about the size of a wooden stake used to hold tomato plants up, he will mark the spot where he saw the bedded fish with a stake (near the bed but not sticking in it). Marking a bed that has a fish on it enables Scroggins to throw to that fish without spooking it. "When you come back in the morning during low-light conditions, you can't see that bed but you can see the stake. I always say, if you can see the fish, the fish can see you. The bigger the fish, the harder they are. So what we like to do is take those tomato stakes and stick them right outside of the bed and mark the bed, then come back the next morning and make a cast to that stake. Nine times out of ten, you'll catch that fish."

For fishing spawning bass, Scroggins's go-to bait is a YUM Craw Pappy in green pumpkin. "If you can see the fish, the beds, the water clarity is good and green pumpkin in clear water is good anytime. For fish that aren't larger than 4 or 5 pounds, using a drop-shot is huge. It works really well."

Scroggins relies on his electronics for offshore structure fishing. When fishing deep water, he hones in on contour lines and fishing breaks.

He recommends covering a lot of water during a tournament, but that doesn't mean you fish fast. "Fish with patience," Scroggins says. He defines that as slowing down your presentation to the fish. "When you feel you have your bait in the strike zone, you need to really slow it down. A lot of your bigger fish are a lot slower to bite. If

you're throwing a Carolina rig, Texas rig, or jig, a lot of times you let it sit there for a while. That makes a big difference. A lot of guys can't do that. It's hard to leave your bait sitting there. I've learned over the last four or five years from experience that when you need to, slow it down. I might fish fifty to a hundred spots a day. Instead of making a hundred casts in there, I'll make fifty, but they are quality casts. Let your bait soak up a bit more."

Randy Howell

Howell is partial to sight fishing for bass during the prespawn, spawn, and postspawn. He equips himself with the right tools to make sight fishing highly effective. First, he makes sure he has the best pair of polarized sunglasses possible. "If you can't see them, you can't catch them," he says.

Knowing that some bass on the spawning beds can get skittish, he goes out of his way to keep some distance between himself and the bass. "I'll move out a little, make a big loop [with the boat], then circle back around and sit out and watch the fish return to the bed. I try to see exactly where the bed is and locate the exact spot the fish is sitting on. You can fish all around a bed and the fish will never get active to bite your bait until you get it right on that very small 'sweet spot.'" The "sweet spot" is about the size of a quarter and is where the bass has laid its eggs on the spawning bed. Bass will look to protect the sweet spot from other egg-eating fish.

"My bait of choice is a 4-inch pink Berkley Power Craw. It's bright and hot pink so that you can see it from far away. The fish are not keying on the color because they like hot pink. I'm keying on that color because I can see it and present the bait properly and see how the fish reacts to it. About 75 percent of the time I can catch them with that pink bait." Seeing the bait helps Howell avoid foul-hooking a bass during a tournament, which can cost you a fish that would normally count toward your total weight.

Howell prefers to fish that bait by making accurate casts right on or near the "sweet spot" and leaving the bait still. "I'll try to get [the bait] to where it's most protective. When the fish moves away, that's the time you can get your bait on that spot without scaring it. As soon as I see the fish look at the bait, seeing something on the bed eating its eggs, I'll start this really subtle shaking of the bait. I'm trying to make the bait quiver right on top of the eggs, like it's down there eating the eggs. That's when you'll see the reaction [from the fish] and know whether he's going to bite or not. If he swims up and looks like he's troubled by it—he starts to invert and stand on his nose or moves around a lot—you know you're really bothering that fish and he's getting nervous. Once you shake it enough, [the bait] will slide out of the spot."

If the bass relaxes once the bait is out of the "sweet spot," you should recast quickly. According to Howell, you don't want to give the fish time to relax. "You want to quickly keep him stirred up as fast as you can get the bait back there and shake it . . . keep bombarding that fish and make him attack [your bait].

"If the spawning bed is in an open area, make a cast past it, sometimes even casting your bait onto the shoreline. That allows you to drag the bait quietly into the water without making any splash and scaring the fish. If the bed is situated between two tree limbs, under a bush, or somewhere you can't drag up to it, that's when you have to make those real subtle pitches." This is where your casting ability comes into play and making accurate casts is key to success. "You want to have a real controlled, subtle pitch to take [the bait] down to the bed without making a big stir."

The ability to catch spawning bass on beds is critical to tournament success. It's not easy to catch bass on beds, it's just easier to locate them. Knowing when a fish is "catchable" is a crucial skill that Howell hones to a science during tournaments. "Usually, bass will make five circles around their [spawning] bed. If they stay away [from the bed], you may as well just move on. If they circle around with their circle getting a little tighter, every time they don't leave the bed as long as before, that is when you know you can lock down on that fish. Once it stops and sits still, then you know that fish is catchable."

If Howell finds that his efforts with the hot pink Berkley Power Craw are not meeting with success, he'll switch to

■ **Make sure your baits are tuned and running well.** DAVID DIRKS

a dark-colored lizard, like a 6-inch black Berkley Power Lizard. It may be that the darker bait looks more threatening to the fish or more like what the fish is used to seeing in the water. You need to keep in mind that when you switch to dark-colored baits when sight fishing on beds, you'll be a little more "blind" to what the bait is doing. A darker bait is just more difficult to pick out at almost any distance. That's why Howell will first use a bright bait pattern, like a hot pink craw, worm, or lizard.

"When I'm using [darker] baits," says Howell, "I'll back off the bed. Then you keep bombarding the fish with that black lizard, letting it do its job. A lot of times they'll bite it after you've moved away from the bed."

When fishing deeper beds or in very windy conditions, Howell will step up to a ⅜-ounce weight. A heavier weight allows the bait to sink faster and get into position on the bed quicker. "I've used weights as heavy as ½ ounce when I've had to. There is no rule on what the weight has to be. I'll rotate between the black lizard and a green pumpkin tube bait or a watermelon craw bait."

Another bait Howell will use on spawning beds is a large bluegill pattern, like a Mattlures Bluegill, which is a swim bait. For bedded fish that are 4 pounds or larger, using a large swim bait like a bluegill will often get them to strike when other baits can't. "It's real heavy, so I put it on a 50-pound-test Firewire Stealth braid line and put it on a big flipping stick."

Howell will swim the bluegill right up to the spawning bed. "It's weighted so that it'll sit on its nose and it looks like it's just standing up on the bed eating eggs. You can let it sit on that spot and start quivering that bluegill. It's a good big-fish bait, and it's also one of the baits I go to to get the really hard fish to bite."

One challenge that pros often have to face when fishing bedded fish is deciding when to give up and find other fish. Most pros will tell you that it's the confidence you have in your ability to find and catch fish that determines just how much time you'll spend trying to catch one big fish. It makes sense—the less confidence you have, the more time you'll be willing to spend on that one big fish you can see. The danger is in the eating up of valuable tournament fishing time. The time you use up on trying to catch one big fish on a bed is something you can't make up for. Highly confident and experienced anglers will spend less time on a big fish they can't entice to bite. They know when it's time for them to move on and find other fish.

Howell's next top presentation is shallow cranking, which he defines as crankbait fishing from the surface to 7 feet of water. "I have probably more shallow-water crankbaits in my boat than any other [lure], with about seven or eight boxes in my boat all the time.

"My number one shallow crankbait is a 0- to 5-foot runner." He uses a Bandit 100 Series shallow crankbait because it has a square lip instead of the standard round lip found on most crankbaits. Howell prefers the square-lipped bait because it ricochets better off of heavy cover like wood and stumps. "You want something that will bang off of cover and not hang up. If I see a lay-down tree with forty limbs on it, all the way out to the boat, I know that somewhere along there, there is a bass ready to eat. The worst thing to do is to throw the wrong-style crankbait into the right place. If you hang [the crankbait] up, you've ruined the whole place and you don't get the chance to get that first-reaction bite. A reaction strike on a crankbait in cover is usually the first cast. That's why that cast needs to be accurate, and the right bait that will bounce off [of cover] and get that strike."

Howell prefers crawfish baits in red and brown, in various shades from darker to lighter. "If you're fishing rocks, wood around rocks, or clay banks, you have to make an educated guess if the fish are feeding on crawfish or shad. I'll start with my confidence colors like a spring craw or one with pearl white with a chartreuse back that has some flash to it like a shad." He'll then let the fish dictate which colors to use based on his results.

His next favorite crankbait is one that rattles, like a Berkley Frenzy, especially during the spring and early summer months. Howell will move on to quieter crankbaits during the middle and late summer, when air temperatures are higher. He will use either lighter shad-imitation colors or a color like fire tiger. "Fire tiger is a good all-around color to use when they're feeding on shad or crawfish." When water conditions are murky or clouded, the fire tiger color shows up very well and has a good flash to it.

"If I'm throwing balsa-type baits up into shallow water around fish that are in wood cover—with the water typically colored, stained, or even muddy—my favorite color is a yellow chartreuse with a black back and an orange belly. That gives [the bait] some flash."

Flipping and pitching give Howell the flexibility he needs to meet a wide variety of tournament conditions. He uses a ½-ounce Lunker Lure Rattleback jig. As for colors, he says, "You really don't have to get too fancy on your colors for a jig as long as you have a black/blue/purple type of color. You can fish that color [combination] almost anywhere you go. If I get into really clear water conditions, then I'll go to a more natural color like green pumpkin or watermelon/crawfish-type colors."

When presenting your jig when pitching or flipping, Howell suggests always putting your bait right where you think the fish is going to be on your first flip. "That's a big key. Lots of times people try to work their way up to the sweet spot and make a little noise and spook the fish. Most of the time on a big fallen tree or big bush in the water, the fish is going to be right in the center of it, right in the thickest and tightest part of the bush or tree. I'll put that jig right in there and let it fall down. Most of the time the bass will bite it on the fall. It's really critical to watch your line as it's falling. They'll have [the bait] in their mouth and you won't even know it." Once you break through the grass and you see your line just stop, or you pick up and feel that mushy tension on the line, setting the hook is your next move. Doing this immediately is critical to boating that fish.

"Hydrilla and milfoil mats are real thick, and usually a jig is not as good there. That's where I'll use a plastic bait with a big tungsten weight; 1 ounce, 1¼ ounces, and 1½ ounces are the three big weights for punching through matted grass." Howell

suggests pitching your bait high into the air and letting it come straight back down so that it plunks through the grass. This method is used by many pros on thick grass mats, hence the name "plunking."

Howell uses a 7-foot, 6-inch heavy-action flipping stick matched with a fast-retrieve reel filled with 65-pound braided line. He also advises using a sturdy, well-made hook when flipping soft plastics on thick grass, since it has to be able to stand up to the pressure of the rod, heavy line, and weights. "You need to use a heavy wire hook that is rated for a heavy braided line."

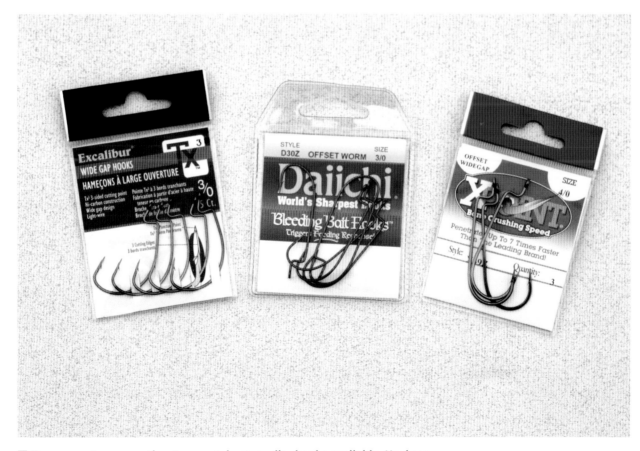

■ Tournament pros use the strongest, best-quality hooks available. Having a big fish break off because of a bad hook could mean thousands of lost dollars.
DAVID DIRKS

It's important to note that Howell ties the braided line directly to his hook and uses a nail knot, which is used for heavy flipping and pitching. "Once I learned that knot, I quit losing fish," says Howell.

Frank Scalish

Deep-cranking summertime structure is one of Scalish's favorite tactics. "When you're looking at deep structure and you're idling over it with your [electronic] locator, there's always something different on a structural element. People get confused when a pro angler says 'structure' or 'cover.' They confuse the two. Structure is not cover. Cover is anything *on* that structure. For example, I find a creek channel and a good drop-off—that's the structure. If there are stumps on it or a rock pile, that's the cover. Anything on that structural element is cover.

"When you're structure fishing, you're looking for some irregularity or some form of cover on that structure. With deep-crankbaiting, it's not just about dropping a buoy on that cover and casting it out and bringing the crankbait back. It's not like that at all. You may have to fish 360 degrees around that structural element to figure out which angle the bass want. Bass definitely choose one angle or another. You're going to pivot 360 degrees around that structural element. The angle of your retrieve can mean success or failure for you. Once you make contact with the fish, you have to remember exactly how you cast [to that fish]. That cast, over and over again, is what is going to catch fish for you."

As to why bass prefer a certain angle of retrieve over other angles, Scalish says, "There are a lot of reasons bass relate to structure and cover, most of which are current-generated. Bass relate to structure and cover in a way that gives them the optimal ambush point for feeding."

He recommends patience while you're looking for structure and cover to fish. "Make sure you're finding the cover on the structure. You may be literally 15 feet from a bag of fish, and if you're in a hurry and just start fishing it, you may miss that bag of fish and never know it." Structure fishing is extremely precise, says Scalish. "It's every bit as precise as flipping. People don't realize that because they don't see it. It's easy to fish what you can see."

Another thing that Scalish says to remember about deep-cranking is that there is such a thing as over-cranking. "Everybody thinks that if you crank it [the bait] superfast, it goes deeper. It's actually the opposite. If you retrieve superfast, it doesn't go as deep. So you want to have a retrieve ratio of about 18 or 19 inches per reel turn."

He also likes to crank the bottom. "I want my crankbait banging into things down there because as it bangs it deflects and turns sideways. It's not running or tracking in a straight line. The deflection of a crankbait triggers more strikes than anything except a pause. I've seen where I've hit an object, paused the crankbait, and the fish is just there. Pauses or deflections are huge [bite] triggering mechanisms."

Scalish describes himself as a "crankbait freak" who keeps his crankbaits simple. "I've got a shad pattern, which means gray back and pearl sides or black back with pearl sides—something that looks like a real shad. The Tennessee #7 shad is probably the best color for shad. Then I have a 'hot' shad pattern, meaning a blue back with a chartreuse belly or a blue-green back, prism-taped sides, and a chartreuse belly. So I have a real shad pattern and a 'hot' shad pattern. Then I go into a crawdad pattern. Crawdad does not necessarily mean it looks like a real crawdad. Basically, it's brown-bone-orange or brown-chartreuse-orange.

"The only variant I have in a color scheme is a perch pattern. I have a real perch pattern that I paint myself. It's a pretty accurate representation of a perch. Basically, I'm throwing that in all my northern smallmouth waters."

Scalish points out that you need to research what the predominant bait colors are for the water you are fishing. "If you're going down to Texas, you better have red with you. What's red? It's a crawdad pattern, and in that part of the world, they [crawdads] are red. You come up north and the crawdads are olive green.

"In dirty, dingy water I'll stick with primarily hot colors or white [as in black back, white belly]. It's a shad pattern, but white shows up [in the water]. Brown shows up in muddy water. Brown and orange is a good muddy water bait-color combination." Scalish has learned over time that experience helps you determine which color combinations are most effective on each body of water you fish.

Flipping is a very popular technique on almost any tournament trail, and it's one that Scalish excels at. "You're fishing visible cover, and it's total combat fishing. It's big lines, big rods, all muscle, and there's no grace except for the actual cast.

"Let's say you're flipping a stump. Did the fish come from the right side or the left side of the stump? Or the back of the stump or the front of the stump? Did he bite it on the way down or when you were jiggling it through the root system? These are things you've got to pay attention to because if he [took the bait] on the way down, it means he's suspending against the stump, in which case you don't want to throw a heavy lure. You want to throw something light that will fall slower, unless, of course, you generated a reaction bite, in which case you want something heavier because it'll rocket by him and he'll attack it. So you have to pay attention to how the bite is coming and where it's coming from: Was he on softwood or hardwood? Was it a willow tree or an oak tree? If you're fishing an area with nothing but flooded willows and every time you come to a piece of hardwood and catch one, why flip the willows?

"I once helped a buddy of mine practice for a local tournament. The lake was known as a flipping lake. It's mostly surrounded by flooded willow trees and willow tops. We ran out and started flipping because that was the bite for sure on the lake. We'd flip these willow bushes and catch little 12½- to 13-inch largemouth. I came up to a piece of hardwood and I flipped in there and caught a 4-pounder. I flipped on the other side of it and caught another one. So we set out to hit every piece of hardwood we could find. Sure enough, every piece of hardwood that we could find, we caught a monster off of it."

Scalish explains it this way: "It's like [fishing] a grass bed. Are they in the hydrilla? The milfoil? Or the eel grass? It's just their preference at the time, and that's what the pattern is. Most of the guys will see all the willows and go, 'I've got to flip the willows.' And they'll catch 1-pounders and be totally happy with that. They may flip 100 yards of willows and hit one hardwood and catch a big one. Then they'll say, 'I told you the willows have them!' My friend did nothing more than run the hardwoods, and he won it."

In terms of flipping baits, Scalish narrows it down to personal preference. "If you knock a fish on the head with it, he's going to bite it. My first choice of flipping baits is a lizard, mostly because hardly anyone throws it. It's sort of the forgotten bait. It's got a lot of movement. The tail moves, the legs move, it just creates a lot of movement. It helps to trigger the bite, so it's a good bait to use if someone rips through with a jig and I can go behind him with a lizard and maybe catch a few fish he didn't get. My go-to colors for lizards are june bug, green pumpkin, and watermelon or red bug."

Scalish's next choice is a jig. "A jig is one of the number one big bass baits ever made. My color selection for jigs is even easier. It'll be black, blue, and purple or green pumpkin. . . . If I go through an area and get a few bites on a lizard, I'll usually go back through with a jig, just to see which one the preference is. Again, when I'm flipping in practice, I'm not hooking the fish." Scalish stresses that the idea with flipping is not to be snagging. "If you're throwing a jig and hanging up all the time, there are probably two problems: Either your weed guard is cut too short or it's too soft. Or the hook is too long or you're using the wrong head style."

Scalish uses a drop-shot as part of his tournament arsenal. "It's a fish-catching tool. I don't see how an angler in this day and age could leave for the water without having a drop-shot rigged. It accounts for so many fish and so many quality fish. You can deep-structure fish with it, you can sight fish with it, you can flip docks with it." His top choices for drop-shotting are 4- and 6-inch Houdini worms and YUM Dingers. He prefers 7- to 7½-foot medium-action spinning rods and thinks that most people tend to drop-shot on too soft of a rod.

"When I fish boat docks, I put the Houdini worm or YUM Dinger on a flipping stick and use 17- or 20-pound line. Same thing when I'm fishing grass. For

■ **Weedless jigs, like these Booyah jigs, are specifically designed to punch through tough vegetation and provoke a reaction bite from bass.** DAVID DIRKS

grass, I'll rig it on braided line and put a 1- to 1½-ounce sinker at the bottom of it to poke holes through the grass. It's not just a finesse technique—it has grown a lot of legs."

Scalish's favorite way to fish is the deepwater finesse style of drop-shotting. "It accounts for 90 percent of the smallmouth I catch and probably 60 percent of the spotted bass I catch. It's a tool. I'm using a 7- to 7½-foot Powell spinning rod with 10-pound-test fluorocarbon. I very rarely go lighter than 10-pound fluorocarbon when I'm drop-shotting because

fluorocarbon doesn't reflect light, so it's almost invisible to the fish." He recommends going to a lighter line only when you need to go to a lighter weight. Scalish encourages anglers to experiment with drop-shotting and to remember it's not just for light-line fishing: "You can wacky rig, Texas rig, and flip heavy grass with a drop-shot."

Scalish himself is always experimenting, such as with the length between his weight and the hook. "I have had situations where I've had the weight down and the hook 3 feet above it, and that's how I caught all my fish. When I lowered the hook closer to the sinker, I didn't get bit because the fish were suspending off the bottom. You want to pay attention to where those fish are in relation to the bottom.

"Make sure your line diameter doesn't exceed your weight's capacity. The whole key with drop-shotting is to be able to feel what it's doing down there [in the water]. If you use too light a sinker with too heavy a line, the line has a tendency to 'float.' It doesn't really float, but you can't feel anything. Therefore, you're not going to be as successful at it. A lot of the bites with drop-shotting are so subtle. Now, obviously, some of the hits are unbelievable, but most are very subtle and soft. If you're bed fishing with a drop-shot, you want the hook to be 3 to 6 inches above the weight.

"If you're fishing for spotted bass or smallmouth, get way above the weight. Largemouth can be 6 to 12 inches above the weight. When drop-shotting grass, what I do is stay in the middle of the pocket. For example, if you're fishing hydrilla, it's going to have huge caverns under the mat. So, you want to figure out where the bass are: Are they underneath the canopy? Or are they relating to the stalks, where it all converges together? That's going to dictate the distance from the weight to the hook."

Jimmy Mason

Flipping a grass lake rates high on Mason's list of tactics that contribute to his tournament success. "I like to approach grass mats looking for contours I would fish if there were no grass on the lake. The fish are going to be in the same structure places, such as creek channel swings, creek channel points, and main lake points. The grass is just the extra cover over the top of the structure. I'll put my trolling motor on a real slow pace and methodically make flips into the vegetation.

"What I'm really looking for in the mats are areas where it's slightly different. You'll see a different coloration of the mats, where you have an area of bright green grass and an area that has a brownish/blackish tint on the top. Those brownish/blackish areas of the grass mat are indicative of voids in the grass area itself. It's a real likely area to find fish in.

"You're also looking for areas with matted vegetation that's come to the top of the water and is starting to fold over onto itself. You want to make short flips with a heavy line like 65-pound braided line with a ¾- to 1¼-ounce tungsten weight and a small bait like a YUM Big Show Craw. It's a very compact bait that doesn't have any appendages that would catch the grass as it falls in. . . . Basically, you're looking for areas of concentrations of fish that are under the [grass] mats. On a grass lake, it's how you win or have high finishes."

When flipping, Mason puts a rubber bobber-stopper on his line before he puts his weight on. "That keeps my weight real close to my bait when I'm flipping in, so it keeps it from hanging up." A bobber-stopper is a small piece of rubber with a hole in it that you simply thread onto your line.

For grass flipping with braided line, Mason prefers to use a fairly soft flipping stick or a light-action flipping stick in a 7½ foot length. As for the reel, "You want to use a high-speed reel so that you can get the fish coming out of the cover." He cranks that reel at 28 inches per turn, so he has the ability to maneuver a fish out of the cover and boat it quickly.

During a tournament, Mason will have at least four rods rigged with flipping baits on his boat and ready to go. If he hooks a fish and boats it, he'll quickly put the fish in the live well, bait and all, and pick up another rod to immediately throw into the water. "This is a technique where the fish really group up tight in the [grass] mats. I want to get another bait back into the hole where I just caught a fish as fast as I can. If I get a bite on the next cast, that fish goes into the live well, hook and all. Then I grab the next rod. To me, it's quicker to have another rod ready to go. I save fifteen to twenty seconds by doing that, and that's critical. When I hit a group of fish, by having four rods ready, I can have four fish in the boat in less than a minute. It's really important when you

Jimmy Mason works a dock during a practice. Docks are consistent producers of fish, especially around release areas. LURENET.COM

hit that first fish, when they are grouped up, to get back in there immediately." Call it "speed fishing," but when every second counts during a tournament, it can make all the difference.

Shallow cranking is the arrow in the Mason quiver. He prefers to go with a square-lipped crankbait for shallow-water cranking because it deflects better off his targets. Square-lipped crankbaits move erratically from side to side as they travel in a straight line, and it's that erratic action that triggers the bites. Mason's main targets are creeks and rivers that have slightly stained water. "I'm looking for wood on flats, wood up the creek, channel bends, and where the flats transition into the channels." He also has his eye out for any cover on that structure like blowdowns, rocks, and especially docks that have fixed poles, not the kind that float.

Mason likes to set up his boat so that he's straight out to the target, whether it's a laydown or a dock, so that his crankbait is making contact as many times as possible. "When I'm cranking a dock, I want my crankbait to hit every pole on the dock. Same thing with the laydown—I want the crankbait to stay in contact with the branches and trunk of the laydown. A lot of your bites when you are shallow cranking are reaction bites. The vast majority of the bites you're going to get are right after your bait comes in contact with an object and deflects off of it." He has learned over time that stained water can make the fish relate tighter to the structure. "It brings them up shallower and puts them on the targets a little better."

Like most pros, when it comes to color, Mason likes to keep it simple. "I pretty much throw two colors: One is a chartreuse root beer with a brown back, chartreuse sides, and an orange belly. The other is a Tennessee shad color, with a black back, white sides, and an orange belly. The only time I'll throw a different color is early in the spring—I'll mix in some reds just because a lot of the crawfish have a reddish tinge to them. I'll throw a goldish orange-red or even a red, but that's the only variation I have with my colors."

Mason uses 14- to 17-pound-test Silver Thread monofilament line. "I definitely use mono instead of fluorocarbon for this technique because the mono floats, so it helps to keep your bait from getting hung up quite as much." He prefers shallow crankbait rods that have a short handle, which allows for more accurate underhand casts, and uses a 6-foot, 9-inch Kistler graphite rod. He also likes 6:3:1-ratio reels that bring in about 29 inches of line per turn.

"Shallow cranking is a really aggressive technique. You're covering a lot of water, and you're aggressively throwing your crankbait at heavy cover. You're aggressively throwing it around high-percentage areas and basically looking for every target you can and making multiple casts. On a prime dock or laydown, I'll pull up my boat and sit there and make fifteen to twenty casts." He points out that many

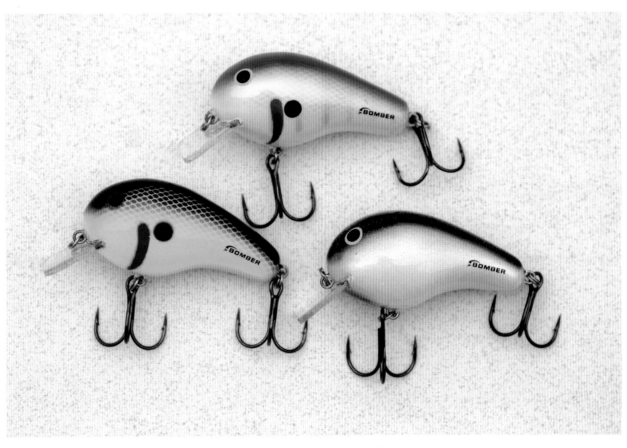

▦ **Most pros try to keep their colors simple. These Bomber B crankbaits represent some of the most popular colors on the pro tour.** DAVID DIRKS

anglers won't target heavy cover with shallow crankbaits because they are afraid to lose their lures. But in a tournament where the stakes are high, it's a technique that is designed to fill the live well for those willing to pursue it.

Bass will relate to cover in different ways depending on the time of day, Mason notes. "I'm thinking about Wheeler Lake, my home lake, where I'm practicing for the Bassmaster Open, and a lot of the fishing I'm doing is shallow cranking. The fish are definitely relating to different parts of the laydowns in the morning versus the

afternoon. The difference is that the TVA [Tennessee Valley Authority] is generating water starting around 12 noon."

Mason takes time to carefully position his boat so that he can make straight casts parallel to the sides of the dock and the pilings. This kind of boat maneuvering is critical to shallow cranking a dock in a tournament. "Until the fish tell me how they are positioned, I'm going to be keeping my angles for my bait as tight to the cover as possible."

He stresses the importance of catching the fish on your first cast. "Your first cast is your high-percentage cast. The fish is sitting there by the target and if you make a cast from a bad angle as you approach the dock, that fish is going to sense that bait. He's going to spin around and change his position and figure out what that bait is. If you wait until you're straight against the target, then you're going to ricochet it off of his face." That's when you'll get that first "reaction bite" that will get you that fish on the first cast. It's a subtle but critical point in tournament fishing. Get your boat into the best position to give you the opportunity to make a cast that is angled for maximum effectiveness. "To me, waiting to make the perfect cast at the right angle is super critical."

The shaky-head technique has taken both tournament and recreational angling by storm in recent years. It's also a tactic that rounds out Mason's competitive arsenal. "I always have two or three rods rigged for shaky-head in my boat. It's a 'check-getting' technique. I use a 4- or 6-inch YUM Houdini worm in green pumpkin— just about as simple as it gets. It's a really effective bait to fish in grass when it's heavily pressured or it's a post–cold front situation, when the fish are outside of the grass and really lethargic. You can fish the sparser grass with this technique. To me, it's most effective around rock and wood. I like to use as light a jighead as possible. The ⅛ ounce is the one I use the most, but if I'm fishing around riprap, I'll drop down to a ¹⁄₃₂ ounce where I can float my worm over the rocks to keep it from getting down

into the cracks and getting hung up. If I'm fishing deeper water, I'll go up to a ³⁄₁₆- or ¼-ounce weight.

"When we were at Clear Lake this year in the Elite Series event, thirteen of the fifteen fish I caught were on a shaky-head. I had a little over 62 pounds, and with the exception of two 4-pounders I caught on a swim bait, everything else came on a ¼-ounce shaky-head in about 25 feet of water, with a 6-inch Houdini worm. I was fishing staging fish, fish that were moving up on the spawning areas. The fish were pretty spooky, but they were also really grouped up. That ¼-ounce head would get down there really fast."

Mason also likes to use as light a line as possible when fishing open water. "I never go over 10-pound test, even when I'm skipping under docks. I use 6-pound test more than any other pound test. I always fish a shaky-head on spinning tackle. I use a 6½-foot Kistler medium/heavy spinning rod. It's a parabolic rod, so that it has an even bend from the midsection to the tip. I always use fluorocarbon with this method. I use 6-pound test probably 75 percent of the time, 8-pound test about 20 percent of the time, and 10-pound test about 5 percent of the time.

"A lot of times when you're casting a shaky-head, you want your bait to fall vertically, whether it's a pier pole, barge tie-up, retaining wall, or bridge pier. By keeping your bail open on the reel, it allows the bait to fall and not pendulum back towards you like you were using a baitcaster. Most of the spinning reel drags are a little better than a lot of baitcasters. So the spinning reel allows you to handle the light line much better."

Mason says that when things get tough at the end of the day and you can't get a bite on anything else, pick up a shaky-head and hit as many docks and pieces of wood on flat, rocky points as you can. "A lot of guys on the second or third day of the tournament will fish outside the off-limits area trying to catch release fish. This is a great way to catch release fish because it's a subtle and great finesse technique."

Sam Swett

Swett is another fan of the shaky-head technique, and he considers it absolutely indispensable for the tournament angler. "Power fishing is starting to go away. The big crankbaiters and Bubba baits are giving way to finesse fishing." He stresses that the increasing popularity of bass fishing and the larger number of tournaments being held on lakes increase the need for more delicate fishing presentations, like the shaky-head technique. It's not uncommon for a lake to have a two- or three-hundred-

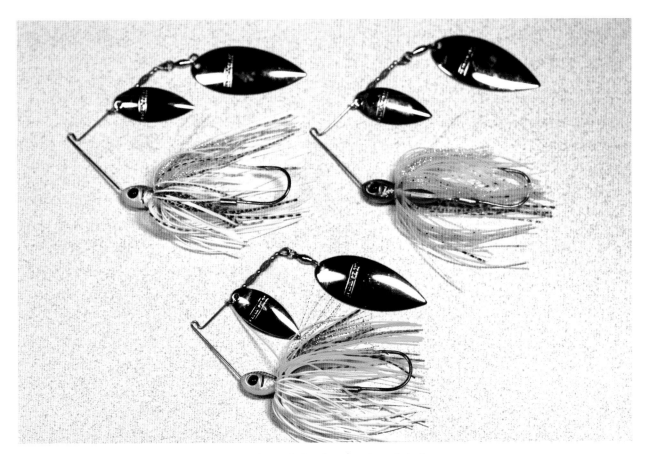

■ **Spinnerbaits remain the tournament pros' top choice for covering a lot of water and searching for bass.** DAVID DIRKS

■ Having a good supply of soft baits is critical for finesse fishing.
DAVID DIRKS

boat tournament week after week during the season. "These fish have seen everything. The very small, finesse-type baits are what will catch fish. I use an All Star 6½- or 7-foot medium-action rod. Faster-taper rods allow you to impart that 'shaky-head' action to the lure effectively."

Swett believes that one of the best things a tournament angler can do is become one of the best casters in the world. "With the lake pressure and the popularity of fishing, pinpoint casting is very, very crucial in this sport. You want to get your baits to where other anglers possibly can't get to. You have to learn how to skip, pitch, and flip baits deep under docks or into heavy cover.

In general, Swett says, "A spinnerbait is a bait that can be fished year-round. It's a locator bait that helps me to find fish. It's a bait that can cover a lot of water and maximize your time if you're not on to anything."

Paul Elias

Throwing deep-diving crankbaits is Elias's "go-to" tactic. "I love to fish water between 8 and 12 feet deep that is close to deeper water. I like a diving bait because I can cover a lot of ground. It's a reaction bait that causes the fish to strike a lot of times. The potential to catch a big stringer is a lot better with a pretty good-sized bait in an area where you're going to run into schools of fish. That's what I'm constantly looking for."

Elias's number one bait choice is a Mann's 20+. "The reason is that bait has a wide lip on it and it goes through cover a lot better than most deep-diving crankbaits. It's a confidence factor because I've caught so many big stringers on it that I know its potential. That's what I'll start with." If that's not working, he'll switch to a deep-diving bait that has a narrow lip and a little wobble that causes the fish to strike. Typically, he'll have at least three different deep-diving crankbaits tied on rods.

Deep-diving crankbaits need to dig into the bottom in order to be effective, says Elias. He is looking for something different on the bottom of the lake—some kind of cover that the bass will use as their "house." "Most of the time I try to make as long a cast as I can, trying to cover more ground and get the bait down. When I feel that bait start to hit something or start to come over something [on the bottom], that to me is a potential place to catch a fish. I start paying closer attention. I hesitate the bait and try to get it to ride over and then speed [the retrieve] up. To me, that's trying to make something that's not real look alive. So I pay real close attention to what that bait is doing on the bottom." When he hooks a fish, Elias also pays close attention to the angle at which the fish took the bait. His next cast is lined up so that it's an exact repeat of the last cast, so casting accuracy is critical.

Again, the angle of presentation can drive your tournament performance. "If you throw 10 feet to the left of a stump or 5

▓ Paul Elias tunes one of his favorite deep crankbaits. By adjusting the lip on the crankbait, he can change its action in the water. DAVID DIRKS

feet to the right of the stump, a lot of times you're not going to get a bite. There's an angle they want that bait to come through, and you can hit that stump from one direction five times and not get a bite. Then you can go around from a different direction and catch one almost every cast. You have to figure those things out.

"There are times when you are going to catch fish suspended on a crankbait or standing trees. If you're fishing the tops of trees, that's just like fishing the bottom—you want that bait digging into the tops of those trees. You want that bait hitting structure all the time, or hitting the cover all the time."

Boat positioning, especially when deep-cranking, is critical in order to get the bait deep enough. "If your cast is 50 yards, you want to have your boat at the most 20 yards from the piece of cover you're trying to hit. It takes that [additional] 30 yards just to get the bait down to that depth in order to come through that cover. A lot of people don't realize that. They'll see a hump and mark it and make a long cast to it. They'll think that crankbait is going to get down there and hit that hump." Of course, they miss the hump by a mile and miss fish that could help them win the tournament.

Elias is well-known for his "kneel and reel," a technique that he perfected and is now used by many tournament anglers. "I'm known for that just because I won the Classic doing that. I found a place on the Alabama River that was one of those

■ Elias demonstrates his now-famous "kneel and reel" technique of getting his crankbait to run deeper. DAVID DIRKS

instinct things that told me there should be fish here. I fished that place three different times before I got a bite on it. I caught a little 12-inch fish. This was during the pre-fish for the Classic. The last day I was there, I hit it one more time." Using a deep-diving crankbait, Elias caught 4- and 5-pound fish on back-to-back casts. Keep in mind that the pre-fish was in September and the tournament was being held in October. Cool weather during the tournament caused the bass to fall back into deeper water; however, some good-sized spotted bass came in shallower and took their place. "In order to get the bait down to where the fish had moved in to about 12 feet of water, I had to make as long a cast as I could. Then I'd stick my rod down into the water up to the reel and get the bait to touch that cover in 12 feet of water." And so the "kneel and reel" technique was born.

He uses a 7-foot, 11-inch rod that has a medium action and likes the longer rod because it allows him to kneel and reel. "I don't like a real wimpy rod. I like one that has some backbone to it with a flexible tip so I can load it up and make a long cast with it." As for reels, Elias prefers a 5:1 gear ratio. "There are times when you want to burn a crankbait, and there are times you want to take it really slow. Normally, a medium retrieve is pretty good with a 5:1 reel. The majority of the time I'm throwing 10- to 12-pound test."

Elias's favorite colors for crankbaits are simple but highly effective. He particularly likes the bluegill color, which is a brown or black back with chartreuse and an orange belly; the crawfish color, which is a black or brown back with an orange belly; and two shad colors: a blue back with chrome and a basic Gray Ghost pattern with a gray back, pearl sides, and a light orange belly. He believes that most bait colors are designed to catch fishermen, not fish, "so when you go into a store and you start looking at all these colors with such a wide variety, to me it's better to buy four of one color that you like instead of buying one of four different colors. You're going to lose crankbaits. If you're not, you aren't throwing them in the right place."

What would Elias use if he needed bait with sheer fish-catching power? "It would be a ⅝- or ¾-ounce lipless crankbait. On grass lakes, I'll throw it on braid and rip it through the grass. I'll use a 7:1-gear-ratio reel and rip the bait through the grass, trying to get reaction strikes out of it."

He also likes to work a lipless crankbait through flooded bushes with braided line. He'll fish it like a worm by pulling the bait along, letting it settle on the bottom, and then pulling it along again. He says it's not something you can do in heavy wood cover, but for lakes with grass and bushes, it's ideal. "It's probably the most versatile bait out there. You can throw it at shoreline cover, out in the middle of the lake, or in grass; you can flip it, pitch it, and swim it. It's just a 'go-to' bait that you've got to have."

Elias says there is seldom a tournament where you're not tying on a jig at some

Lipless crankbaits, like these Cordell Super Spots, represent some of the most popular color combinations. DAVID DIRKS

point and throwing it. "I'm pretty flexible on the colors. I use jigs that are black and blue and green pumpkin. Most of the time I'll throw a ½-ounce jig."

He'll fish a traditional jig the same way he fishes a plastic worm. "I'll throw it out there and let it go to the bottom and work it back to the boat, picking it up and letting it fall. I'll swim it through grass. I'll swim it by bushes and docks. In deep water, I'll rip it off the bottom really quick, just by turning the reel handle fast and then letting it swim back down to the bottom. On certain lakes like Kentucky Lake or Toledo Bend, there are times when the bass want that jig ripped up off the bottom with your rod."

CHAPTER SIX

The Business of Tournaments

The thing that prevents most anglers from getting access to BASS or FLW tournaments is the cost. Entry fees are in the thousands. Then you need equipment, and lots of it. Many pros bring anywhere from twenty-five to forty rods with them to each tournament. And don't forget the bass boat, which with even a basic engine and electronics package is going to set you back $25,000 to $35,000. On top of all that, you can throw in the extra travel costs like gas, hotel, and food, in addition to those "emergency" repairs that show up at the wrong time.

The cost of operating on an eleven-or-more-tournament trail can run over $100,000 per year. Unless you have a dream job that allows you unlimited time off with a fat salary, it's a real reach without help. That's where sponsors come into play. Getting sponsors is not easy but not necessarily impossible either. It takes good, old-fashioned hard work and staying power to get and keep sponsors. But don't take my word for it—listen to what the professionals have to say.

Scott Rauber, a leading marketing consultant who specializes in helping anglers develop strategies for acquiring and keeping sponsors, knows just how tough it is to get them. "You've got to leave the fishing industry and look outside it for sponsors. The fishing industry as a whole is hammered for sponsors." He notes that the fishing industry is asked not only to sponsor tournament anglers, but also provide goods and services to an endless line of community groups, fishing clubs, and local and regional tournaments. "Look for someone outside the industry for sponsorship," he advises.

Rauber strongly recommends that anglers prepare a game plan outlining how they can help a potential sponsor land more business. It's not enough to say, "Slap your logo on my shirt and truck." You have to aggressively put together a game plan to actually help them attract business and new customers.

Network, network, network, Rauber advises. "Talk to as many people as you can to attract sponsorship. Don't leave anyone out. You never know who's going to be your next sponsor. Your most unlikely candidate might just become your full boat sponsor."

■ Part of being a pro tournament angler is helping sponsors sell more tackle. Jimmy Mason works with a customer during a tackle trade show. LURENET.COM

Your fishing success is not as important as everybody makes it out to be. Placing in the top five or ten in local tournaments doesn't earn you the right to get a sponsor. Businesses don't care who you beat and how many times you beat them, says Rauber. What they care about is whether or not you can help them sell more product.

The business side of tournament fishing is marketing and media, says bass pro Frank Scalish. Your tournament performances only enhance your potential media coverage. You need to have some marketing savvy in order to make it in the big leagues of BASS or FLW tournaments, and you have to be very comfortable and articulate when you are dealing with the media. "There are a lot of guys who can get media coverage because they can catch fish. But as soon as the media lights are turned on or a microphone is shoved in their face, they're at a loss," says Scalish.

"If you think you're going to get a sponsor because you tell him that you can fish well, you have another thing coming," Scalish points out. "Everyone in the free world who wants a sponsor, that's the first thing out of their mouth." A sponsor is

■ Frank Scalish signs an autograph while working a trade show.
LURENET.COM

going to ask you how many boats or how many rods you've sold.

You will also need the skill of being able to deal with a wide variety of personalities. You'll have to learn to deal with abrasive people with a smiling attitude. Whenever you're on the road representing your sponsor, your sponsor's reputation always comes first. Run into someone who rubs you the wrong way while on a sponsor trip or show? Smile and make the best of it. If you handle the situation badly, it reflects on your sponsor. "No matter how crappy your day is or how bad you feel at the time," explains Scalish, "you need to be in your 'A' game when it comes to your sponsors."

Terry Scroggins dedicates about 250 days a year to tournament fishing and helping his sponsors. He believes you need to make sure you are always adding value to your sponsor relationships, and that starts by making yourself available to them whenever they need you. "I tell my sponsors that I'll give them 365 days. If you need me, call me and I'll be there unless I'm already booked somewhere else," say Scroggins. He feels that it is a

■ **Terry Scroggins works a tackle trade show as part of his sponsor responsibilities. He spends 250 days a year on the road, many of them at shows like this.** LURENET.COM

major mistake for an angler to try to limit the number of days available for a sponsor. "If you want to get paid, you've got to work. They are not going to send you money to stay at home. Your job is to promote their product," he adds.

Almost every pro puts a quarterly or annual report together that demonstrates their value to their sponsors. This report includes how many events they attended that promoted their sponsors and how many advertising "impressions" were made during the course of the quarter or year. If you get sponsors at any level of tournament play, whether local or national, you need to show them the number of times you've directly or indirectly helped their business.

It's also critical to stay in regular contact with your sponsors. Scroggins says that the biggest mistake a tournament angler can make is to get sponsorship funding and then not stay in regular contact with them. Don't take your sponsorship for granted and put it on automatic pilot.

Finally, don't overlook the smaller businesses in your area as potential sponsors. The combined contributions of smaller local businesses can add up to a considerable amount of support for tournament fees and other related expenses.

Bass Pro Biographies

Statistics are current to December 31, 2007.

■ Tournament fishing is physically demanding. Maintain a good workout routine while preparing for tournaments. DAVID DIRKS

Paul Elias

Hometown: Laurel, Mississippi
Bassmaster Classic titles: 1
Times in the Bassmaster Classic: 14
Total (BASS and FLW) entries: 332
Combined career winnings: $962,269
Web site: www.indepthfishinglessons.com

Elias recalls that in his early teens, he seemed to have a knack for catching fish. "I always loved to fish. Every time I went with my friends, it always seemed like I caught more fish and bigger fish. So everybody kind of looked up to me and wanted to go fishing with me. I was very poor coming up in life. I didn't have a boat, so I had to rely on other people for a boat."

After finishing college, Elias took a job offshore and worked until he had enough saved for his first bass boat. After convincing his first sponsor to help him with expenses, he signed up for the American Bass Fisherman (ABF) tour. In his first two years, Elias placed well, finishing in the top ten. Eventually, he found his way to the Bassmaster tour and kept going from there.

■ **Paul Elias**
LURENET.COM

■ **Randy Howell**
LURENET.COM

Randy Howell

Hometown: Springville, Alabama
Times in the Bassmaster Classic: 7
Total (BASS and FLW) entries: 218
Times in the money: 90
Combined career winnings: $912,053
Web site: www.randyhowell.com

While many tournament pros got their starts as young recreational anglers, Howell took a different track. "My mom and dad bought a small fishing marina when I was eleven years old on Lake Gaston on the North Carolina–Virginia border." While devoting most of his time to fishing, Howell also worked the marina tackle store and the boat rental business at the same time. "I started guiding when I was twelve years old. I was actually getting paid for taking guys out on fishing trips."

Now, years later, he still gets plenty of mail and e-mail from folks that he guided as a young teenager. "My dad was a tournament fisherman and wanted to be a bass pro himself." His father, recognizing the natural fishing talent his son possessed, did everything he could to provide Randy with the opportunities to fish tournaments. "I fished local tournaments as a teenager and then fished the Redman tournament trail at the age of sixteen." At the time, Howell was the youngest to qualify for the Redman regional tournament. "I just never thought about doing anything else. I had no other plan of attack other than being a professional fisherman."

Jimmy Mason

Hometown: Rogersville, Alabama
Total (BASS and FLW) entries: 95
Times in the money: 20
Combined career winnings: $57,254
Web site: www.jimmymasonbasspro.com

Growing up about a mile from bass-filled Wheeler Lake in Alabama gave Mason the place he needed to learn the craft of bass fishing. His father, a local tournament fisherman, gave Jimmy his introduction to tournament fishing for bass. "I grew up fishing. I learned to walk during a family fishing/camping trip. I'd see Daddy come home after a tournament and talk about what he had won. So that's what I wanted to do. I wanted to be like Dad. As I got older, I'd fish with him and got the taste of tournaments by fishing team tournaments with him. I just got bit by the bug."

■ Jimmy Mason
LURENET.COM

■ **Frank Scalish**
LURENET.COM

Frank Scalish

Hometown: Cleveland Heights, Ohio
Times in the Bassmaster Classic: 1
Total (BASS and FLW) entries: 84
Times in the money: 26
Combined career winnings: $189,330
Web site: www.osiproseries.com/
frank-scalish

Scalish was about fourteen years old when he decided that competing in bass tournaments was something he just had to do. "I told my father that tournament fishing was what I wanted to do for a living. Of course, he laughed. Back then, it wasn't a living. It was glorified club tournament fishing." He fished his first bass tournament at age sixteen and took second place. Soon he was entering local tournaments throughout Ohio and gaining valuable tournament experience.

After getting a degree in marketing from Ohio State, Scalish established himself in advertising but the tournament bug persisted. "I started my own ad agency just so I could take time off to fish whenever I wanted to. And it wasn't just for bass. I fish for everything that swims." After his dad passed away in 2001, he decided to enter the pro tour by competing in a qualifier. "And I never turned back since. I qualified in 2001, and 2002 was my first full year as a pro and I won rookie of the year."

Terry Scroggins

Hometown: Palatka, Florida

Times in the Bassmaster Classic: 4

Total BASS entries: 82

Times in the money: 56

Career BASS winnings: $926,115

"I've been in a boat since I was two years old," says Scroggins. "I used to go out with my dad. I've been fishing my whole life. I started fishing bass tournaments with my dad when I was twelve or thirteen years old. When I turned sixteen, I started fishing tournaments on my own with other guys. There always had to be someone eighteen years old or older in the boat in order to meet the requirements."

In his second BASS tournament, Scroggins won handily and started his career by winning $50,000. Now, ranked one of the top twenty-five bass tournament anglers in the world, he's looking forward to many more years of competitive bass fishing.

▍ **Terry Scroggins**
DAVID DIRKS

Sam Swett
COURTESY SAM SWETT

Sam Swett

Home: Covington, Louisiana
Times in the money: 26
Combined career winnings: $230,499

"I started fishing when I was too young to remember," recalls Swett. "I remember the very first bass I caught. We had a farm and a three-acre pond. I was seven years old and was using a Zebco 202. Ever since then, I was caught into fishing." In 1981, as a high school graduation present, his parents gave him a guided bass-fishing trip on Toledo Bend. Little did Swett know at the time that the guide they hired was with the legendary Jack Hanes, who was the second Bassmaster Classic winner in the very early days of BASS under Ray Scott. "He got me hooked into the tournament aspect of fishing."

A few years later, in 1988, with encouragement from Hanes, Swett entered his first bass tournament as an amateur. With that, he started beating some of the pros on the tour. Hanes pointed out the obvious to Swett: If you can beat some of the best pros in these tournaments, you could do well as a pro yourself. His continued success led Swett to pick up significant sponsors and go full-time on the tournament trail.

Helpful Tournament Forms

This form is designed to help you organize your practice time and keep track of the key spots you need to find before the tournament begins.

Category Spots	Practice Day 1	Practice Day 2	Practice Day 3
Category A Spots			
Category B Spots			
Category C+ Spots			
Limit-Out Spots			
Notes			

This form is designed to help you constantly monitor and improve your skill levels as a professional tour angler. Learning is a constant requirement for a successful tournament pro.

Top Strengths	Mid-Strengths	Weaknesses	Plan for Enhancement/Improvement
Your best presentations/tactics where you have *exceptional* ability, skill, and confidence. These are your "go-to" tactics. Keep learning how to do them even better!	Secondary strengths with moderate level of ability, skill, and confidence.	Low confidence areas with low skill level and little expertise. Be honest with yourself–even the best pros admit their weaknesses.	How can you develop or enhance the skill levels of your strengths, mid-strengths, and weaknesses? What can you do during the off-season to build strength in all areas?

About the Author

David Dirks is a freelance outdoor writer. He writes a weekly outdoor column for the *Times Herald-Record* in New York State and has written for several outdoor magazines, including *American Angler, New York Game & Fish*, and *Boating on the Hudson*. He is a member of the New York State Outdoor Writers Association and the Metropolitan Outdoor Writers Association. He is also the host of the DirksOutdoors Radio show on WTBQ.com. He lives in Orange County, New York, with his wife, Christine, and four growing children.

■ **David Dirks** COURTESY DAVID DIRKS

Get more secrets from the pros in these fine Pro Tactics™ books:

Pro Tactics™: Bass

Pro Tactics™: Catfish

Pro Tactics™: Ice Fishing

Pro Tactics™: Muskie

Pro Tactics™: Northern Pike

Pro Tactics™: Panfish

Pro Tactics™: Steelhead & Salmon

Pro Tactics™: Tackle Repair & Maintenance

Pro Tactics™: The Fishing Boat

Pro Tactics™: Walleye